Women and the Word: Sermons

Women and the Word: Sermons

edited by
HELEN GRAY CROTWELL

FORTRESS PRESS   PHILADELPHIA

COPYRIGHT © 1978 BY FORTRESS PRESS

Library of Congress Cataloging in Publication Data

Main entry under title:

Women and the word sermons.

    1. Sermons, American—Women authors. I. Crotwell, Helen Gray, 1925-
BV4241.W65   252′.00973   77-78627
ISBN 0-8006-1318-X

6439H77   Printed in the United States of America   1–318

Contents

v

Preface

There are people who have seldom, if ever, heard a woman preach. When asked for reactions to these words—*sermon, black preacher, white male preacher,* and *woman preacher*—people in an ecumenical congregation responded quickly to all the terms, with the exception of *woman preacher.* The mention of woman preacher brought pauses and surprised looks. One man, whose personal experience of hearing women preach was positive, used the terms *sensitive to issues, richness, grace, engages congregation.* He then said, somewhat facetiously: "A woman preacher is like a dog walking on its hind legs. You don't expect it, and are surprised that a dog can perform this difficult feat at all" (a variation on a quotation from Boswell's *Life of Dr. Johnson).*

Since people have few opportunities to hear a woman preach, hesitancy in responding to the term *woman preacher* is not surprising. Even the recent wars, which opened many of the standard male vocations to women, did not affect the pulpit, for ministers had draft exempt status. When you consider the traditional images and expectations of preaching and the traditional images of woman, it is not surprising that there have been so few women preachers. Women have been taught by our culture and by the church to be nonassertive, submissive, soft spoken, demure; they are supposed to be nonrational, emotional creatures. Women have also been taught to be nurturing, caring, hearing, enabling, sensitive persons who have the ability to empathize. The pulpit is seen (by the white upper- and middle-class churches) as a place of power and authority, where the word is preached in a forceful, rational, objective manner. The qualities women bring to the church are said to be best suited for other aspects of ministry, but not for the pulpit.

Now that more and more churches are ordaining women, the question of women in the pulpit is being faced by the church in general with fear and excitement, and very specifically and directly by women who see preaching as an important dimension of our ministry. We are becoming more certain that obedience to God involves us in the proclamation of the good news. We are becoming more confident of our ability to preach.

Women are very aware of the power and authority which resides in the person who has the privilege and responsibility of preaching. We are fearful of being seduced by this power, becoming separated from the laity, and forgetting that this power and authority comes from and rests in God. Both men and women, clergy and laity, have been disturbed by the abuse of power and authority by some of the members of the Christian community. The destructive use of the pulpit is reflected in the warning, "Don't preach at me."

Both men and women are discovering that preaching which incorporates the so-called feminine qualities of caring, hearing, healing, and enabling is nonauthoritarian and provides opportunities for communication which are in keeping with our understanding of God's action in Jesus Christ. The Incarnation is an affirmation that the Word became flesh, not just mind. Broadening the depth and dimension of the sermon to include not only rational and logical thought, but also images, concepts, and stories which stretch people's minds and capture their hearts will provide a vehicle for the Word which became flesh.

The pioneering aspect of women preaching has positive and negative dimensions for the church and for women. Churches which open their pulpits to women may well hear the word of God come to them in a new and different way.

The Spirit is always finding new ways to communicate the old, old story. Until a congregation is at home with a woman in the pulpit, some of their responses can be disquieting to us: "You have such a lovely voice." "You are too cute to be a preacher." "I always like my minister to have good-looking legs." Once congregations have the opportunity to hear women preach, the "feat" will not seem so unusual, and women preachers will be seen as persons, not oddities.

This collection of sermons is evidence that women have more than one style and more than one message. Some women are keenly aware that they are developing forms and styles of preaching which will become models for other ministers, especially for women. Having so few women as models or guides as we learn to preach is both frightening and challenging. We have space to develop a personal style which is in harmony with who we are. The content of the sermon is informed by our theology, our understanding of the gospel and the world. The style and structure of the sermon is formed and shaped by our talents and abilities. Knowing that there is no one way, no best way to preach enables women to discover and develop our unique styles and methods. We can experiment as we learn to preach. Such experimentation happens more readily with the support of a group which responds honestly, critically, and lovingly.

Women who are struggling to develop methods of communicating the gospel through the sermon are faced with some difficult questions. Is the style, content, form, and delivery of the sermon different for men than for women? How can women proclaim the good news using a language developed by a patriarchal structure? Can a language be found which will be inclusive of all God's children? What responses can we make to some people's anger at seeing a woman in the pulpit? Will our enthusiasm to bring so-called feminine qualities to preaching blind us to our limitations and to the value of all other styles of preaching?

Some of these questions are addressed directly and indirectly in this collection of sermons; other questions are also faced. All of these sermons were preached in a specific worshipping community. We wanted the sermons to be as they were preached, so we did not abbreviate them in order to include a larger number. We received many excellent sermons, more than could be included in this book. The selection of the sermons from those available was difficult and was made to be representative of the diversity of the women, both ordained and lay, who are deeply involved in the work of the church.

This collection will be helpful for all ministers—male and female, beginners and old-timers. Because of the content of the sermons, the concerns and issues which are addressed, this collection will be a valuable resource for clergy and laity as a devotional book and as a resource book for theological reflection. One of the easiest ways to read theology is to read sermons.

This book was made possible by the cooperation and support of many people. I would like to express special appreciation to Rachel Davies and to Fortress Press for vision, interest, and support; to all the women whose prompt response made possible this important publication, especially those whose sermons did not get included, only because of the limitation of space; to Robert T. Young, minister to Duke University, who helped me find time in a heavy schedule to edit this book; to Jeanette Stokes and Helen Neinast, who spent much time and energy in sharing the responsibility for the editing; to Brenda Sampson, who assumed major responsibility for typing the manuscript, and also to Jackie Andrews; to Sally Overby and Nancy

Rosebaugh for helping with the proofreading; to two groups of women—the Women in Ministry class of Duke Divinity School and the Women Doing Theology group of the Duke University Parish Ministry, who have learned to work cooperatively and collectively and have given me support for all of my ministry, and who have been especially helpful in discussing this collection; and finally to the Duke University Parish Ministry Staff and many of the faculty members of the Divinity School, who suggested names of women to submit sermons and shared of their experiences in editing a book.

HELEN GRAY CROTWELL

Duke University
Durham, North Carolina
Pentecost 1977

Nancy A. Hardesty

"Just as I Am"

Isaiah 43:1–9

My mother's mother was a saintly Christian woman. She and my grandfather were among the founders of the Christian and Missionary Alliance Church I attended as a teenager. Her Bible was her constant companion. One year I shared her bedroom, and every night I would drift off to sleep hearing her praying in the dark. She told me about visions she had, of Jesus and of angels, and I believed her.

I was her only granddaughter. And yet I never felt that she loved me, loved me as I am for who I am. I can remember her, in exasperation over sibling rivalries and childish insubordination, calling me a "witch" and praying God to deliver me from demonic powers. She was always advising me what I had better do if I did not want to become even more evil and end up in hell.

Out of this milieu, my view of God was formed. God, it seemed, did not love me; in fact, most of the time God didn't even like me! After all, I was a basically evil person who couldn't possibly do anything right. My grandmother's warnings were reinforced by the hymns we sang in church. Remember them?

Amazing grace, how sweet the sound,
That saved a *wretch* like me.

Or,

> Alas, and did my Savior bleed,
> And did my Sovereign die?
> Would he devote that sacred head
> For such a *worm* as I?

Eventually I became an Episcopalian. Parts of the liturgy
confirmed my earlier perceptions. We often used a prayer of
confession which affirmed that we were "miserable offend-
ers," and that "there is no health in us." I recently read a
pamphlet which summarized this type of theological thinking. The author declared: "We deserve nothing, earn nothing, merit nothing." My internalization of that kind of thinking was "We are nothing. I am nothing."

I remember ministers trying to make the distinction that
"God hates the sin but loves the sinner." Yet I knew myself
to be sinful through and through. I understood about God's
grace and redemption through Christ's death on the cross. In
a way it only reinforced my idea that God didn't really like
me. God accepted me only when I was hid in Christ, covered
by Christ's blood. God loved Christ, but not me.

The darker side of this image of God was my perception of
God as someone who was always on the lookout to catch me
doing something wrong; someone who just waited to see me
trip and fall; someone who punished people for not keeping
rules impossible to keep.

Erich Fromm in *The Art of Loving* suggests that there are
several different concepts of God. One he calls "patriarchal." The patriarchal God is one who makes demands, estab-
lishes laws and principles, is just and strict, who punishes
and rewards, whose love is conditional on obedience, who
prefers some children to others. Fromm contrasts this with
what he calls a "matriarchal" concept of a God who is
all-protective, nourishing, accepting; whose love is uncondi-

tional, whose love extends equally to all children, whose forgiveness and offer of salvation are unlimited.

I find elements of both images in Scripture. In both Old and New Testaments one finds God pictured as a Father who disciplines his children. As the Book of Hebrews says: *"For the Lord trains the ones that he loves and he punishes all those that he acknowledges as his sons.* Suffering is part of your *training;* God is treating you as his *sons"* (Heb. 12:6–7 JB). The images of patriarchy are clear. God's treatment is strict and severe, reward is conditional on submission. God is the shepherd who uses rod and staff to give wayward sheep a whop across the hindquarters.

In Psalm 23, however, God is pictured as the shepherd who uses rod and staff to comfort the sheep, who pours healing oil on the sheep's wounds. Our Scripture lesson for today (Isa. 43:1–9), speaks of God loving us unconditionally just because that God created us, formed us, redeemed us. The prophet goes on to use distinctly maternal, matriarchal images of God. In chapter 49, verse 15, God declares:

> Can a woman forget her sucking child,
>> that she should have no compassion on the
>> [child] of her womb?
> Even these may forget,
>> yet I will not forget you.

In chapter 66, God again says:

> At her breast will her nurslings be carried
> and fondled in her lap.
> Like [children] comforted by [their] mother
> will I comfort you.   (vv. 12–13 JB)

Isaiah speaks of God who gathers sons and daughters from the ends of the earth; Jesus speaks of a God who sweeps the entire house looking for that one lost coin, that one lost soul (Luke 15:8–10).

As I came to see this multiplicity of images in the Bible, I came to realize that God truly does love me *as I am*. God loves you *as you are*—for three reasons, I believe.

First, we are made by God in God's image. We are icons of God, the only living representations of God. God gave birth to us; we are God's children. We may choose to deface that image; to ruin ourselves in body, mind, and soul; to renounce our parentage. Parental images in Scripture are meant to convey relationship; we may break that relationship. But God continues to love us, each one of us. Our call to worship today was taken from Psalm 136:26 (JB):

> Give thanks to the God of Heaven,
> [God's] love is everlasting!

The last phrase is a refrain throughout the Psalm, "God's love is everlasting." God reiterated this affirmation to Jeremiah (31:3): "I have loved you with an everlasting love; therefore I have continued my faithfulness to you."

Second, God demonstrated that love in the Incarnation, in Jesus the Christ. It was love for us that motivated God to come to earth in human form. Love for us led Jesus to the cross. Love for us raised Jesus from the dead. God has done all the initiating to restore a loving, harmonious relationship between us.

Relationships between persons are often difficult. All of us have experienced these difficulties, I'm sure. Have you ever experienced "unrequited love"? Have you ever been interested in getting to know someone who gave you ambiguous, double messages, who played "hard-to-get"? God does not treat us like that. God does not play games with us. God does not offer us a relationship and then make us jump hurdles or bow and scrape for it. All we have to do is accept that offer; all we have to do is say Yes to God's offer of love, forgiveness, and acceptance. On the other hand, neither is God like another type of human friend who overwhelms you. Have you ever had an acquaintance who was over-eager to be your friend, who constantly plied you with invitations and gifts? God is not like that. God's gifts are distributed without discrimination. Sun and rain shower on good and bad alike. God neither whips us nor bribes us. God simply offers us a choice of accepting or rejecting relationship. The choice is ours.

This point became clearer to me as I worked on my doctoral dissertation which concerned nineteenth-century American feminism and the revivalism of Charles Grandison Finney. Finney's theology was in sharp contrast with that of earlier Calvinist revivalists. These earlier men believed that some people were elect and some damned, regardless of their individual choices and actions. They urged participants in their revivals to pray, study Scripture, repent, do good works in order to find out whether or not they were among the elect, to strive for a conversion experience which might or might not come to them; to wait and see. God knew but appeared to withhold the information. One had to coax God into disclosure. Finney preached a quite different gospel. He said salvation (conversion) was available to all. "Religion," he said, "is something to *do*, not something to *wait for*." Finney stressed human freedom, our ability to choose. It is not that we "cannot" find salvation, find relationship with God; it is that we are "unwilling." God offers us a choice; the choice is ours.

Third, God's love for us is apparent not only in the offer of salvation, of the restoration of right relationship, but also in the way God works with us to bring us again to the fullness of that image in which we were created. We are the children of God and yet God's goal for us is not simply the restoration of that relationship but also growth to adulthood, to maturity. Sometimes, it seems to me, the parental images in Scripture have been used to keep us in perpetual childhood. And God does nourish us, nurse us, feed, clothe, and cuddle us, support us as we learn to walk and talk, interact with us as we study and develop, counsel us in our decision-making, draw us out and drive us deeper. The goal, however, is to help us grow into maturity, to develop the mind of Christ, to become adult. Thus God is not threatened by our independence, by our questions, by our groping decision-making.

God loves us as we are, and as we are becoming. God bears us as parents give birth to a child; God comforts us and disciplines us; God stands beside us as a friend; God encourages us to ever grow toward maturity, toward perfection. God loves us as we are becoming.

An old familiar song makes the same point. Let us sing it together, not as a hymn of invitation to others, but as our own prayer of response to God's love:

> Just as I am, without one plea,
> But that thy Blood was shed for me,
> And that Thou bidd'st me come to thee,
> O Lamb of God, I come, I come.
>
> Just as I am, thou wilt receive,
> Wilt welcome, pardon, cleanse, relieve;
> Because thy promise I believe,
> O Lamb of God, I come, I come!
>
> Just as I am; thy love unknown
> Has broken every barrier down;
> Now to be thine, yea thine alone,
> O Lamb of God, I come, I come!

O God, we come to you. We thank you for your love. We draw strength from that love for the tasks of this day. We love you in return. Help us this day to share our love with others who do not know or cannot feel your love. Amen.

Jeanette Stokes

"Jesus, Son of David, Have Mercy on Me"

Mark 10:46–52

One November afternoon I stood in front of the Durham County Courthouse in a vigil against capital punishment. It was so cold that my woolen coat and furry gloves hardly kept me warm. There would have been little in that scene to remind me of the story of blind Bartimaeus were it not for one strange fellow who drew my attention. Downtown Durham has a self-appointed crier, a weatherbeaten man who walks the streets, morning to night, chanting rhythmical phrases. On this particular day in November the message he brought to our small band of vigilers was: "They killed somebody, we gonna kill them. They killed somebody, we gonna kill them." I recognized this man from having once worked downtown, and I remembered watching folks nod at him, shake his hand, and comment on his rhymes. I knew he would not hurt anyone, and the fervor with which he spoke made little more of an impression upon me than the loud buses on the street in front of the courthouse. Some of the people with me, though, were unfamiliar with this character and were alarmed by his noisy presence. One young man tried to engage him in a conversation about capital punishment. I explained to my companions that the fellow always went up and down the street hollering and that they need not be concerned.

Later I recalled other phrases I had heard the man chant.

They were often religious in nature: "If you don't love God, God's gonna get you. If you don't love God, God's gonna get you." It occurred to me that I would have paid no more attention to him had he been shouting Bartimaeus's plea: "Jesus, Son of David, have mercy on me. Jesus, Son of David, have mercy on me." So much of what goes on right in front of me I do not hear. I pay little more attention to the noisy people of the world than the crowd paid to Bartimaeus in Jericho.

Mark's story of the blind beggar is not only about the coldness of the crowd which followed Jesus around. It is about God and what we can expect of God. There was a lot of noise in Jericho that day. There were enough people with Jesus alone to cause a small ruckus. Bartimaeus himself was not an unusual sight. Blind beggars were as common to the ancient Middle East as lampposts are to Main Street. I don't comment on every lamppost I see. What is a little unusual is that in all the noise and the crowd Jesus heard Bartimaeus, stopped, and entered into his life. Mark does not tell us why Jesus heard Bartimaeus, but we *can* guess what Mark is getting at. He is saying that God hears us. We do not know exactly why, but God does. Not only that, God comes to us. I heard that fellow hollering at the vigilers, but I ingored him and told everyone else to do likewise. God is not like that. God hears us and comes to us.

Several months ago I was talking with Bob Osborn over in the Duke Religion department about God's hearing us. Dr. Osborn said, "Yèa, it is just like Exodus." I said, "What?" He said: "Look it up. It says God heard the children of Israel crying out." So, I looked it up:

> Then the Lord said, "I have seen the affliction of my people who are in Egypt, and have heard their cry because of their taskmasters; I know their sufferings, and I have come down to deliver them out of the hand of the Egyptians."
>
> (Exod. 3:7–8)

"I . . . have heard their cry . . . I know their sufferings." It is true that God had a whole lot to say about things in Exodus. God said a few words to Moses and a few words to Aaron. God did speak, but first of all, God heard. We place so much emphasis on God's talking all the time: God's word on this, and God's word on that. It seems like we think that when we talk we are like God. God did not talk all the time. The Bible says, sometimes, God heard.

This business about hearing is very important to me. I am a very sound sleeper. My apartment mate makes me put the telephone, which is attached to the wall in my room, out in the hall at night. She claims I sleep through the telephone's ringing. I cannot prove it one way or the other, since I never hear it. I suppose some of you have children. I do not. I understand that when you have a baby, your ears become so well-tuned that you wake up to the baby's whimpering in the middle of the night. I would guess it is as true of fathers as it is of mothers. I believe God is like that. God hears my whimpering, my crying, your crying. Creation groans, and God hears. Bartimaeus cried out, and Jesus heard him.

Have you ever had a conversation with somebody and tried to work out an idea that is not yet well-formed in your own mind? This happens often to me when I am trying to write a theology paper. If the person you are talking with is bored, you never get anywhere, except maybe embarrassed. If, however, by some strange magic, he or she gets an inkling of what you are trying to say, sometimes you are able to work out your idea. That is what it means to be heard.

My father died last February. I do not like to talk about it much but I do try to deal with it every now and then. A few days ago I was talking with someone and mentioned my Dad. The person I was with picked up on the reference and asked if I wanted to talk about my Dad some more. I burst into tears. Without my even knowing I wanted to be heard, I was.

A whole scared part of me was able to come out for a little while. God hears us, and sometimes, just sometimes, we are able to hear one another. It is as though we hear one another into being.

It does not help much if someone hears you and does not let you know about it. When one preaches to a stonefaced congregation, it is very hard to tell if they hear or not. A blind friend of mine claims he can tell if a congregation is with him even though he cannot see their faces. How does he know if he is heard? How do we know that God hears us? How did Bartimaeus know Jesus heard him? I think I can answer the last question. Jesus responded—he became a part of Bartimaeus's life, and I really like the way he did it. Jesus had style. Judging from some of the other miracle stories, healing Bartimaeus was standard operating procedure. Jesus could have zapped Bartimaeus and kept right on going, but instead, he chose to get involved with the blind man. There was no razzle-dazzle about Jesus' approach to Bartimaeus. He did not overwhelm him with his power and authority. He gave Bartimaeus a part in his own healing and preserved the blind man's integrity by asking, "What do you want me to do for you?" Now Jesus was not stupid and he was not playing games. Everyone could see that Bartimaeus was blind, or at least half blind, but Jesus gave Bartimaeus the opportunity to make the request himself. God does not just run over us. God calls us out to be the people God created us to be.

When Jesus came to save the world, he identified not with the powerful, but with the weak. He touched people's lives, simple people's lives, and treated them with dignity. He even asked a blind man, "What do you want me to do for you?" Through his hearing and his caring, he healed people, and he empowered people to heal one another.

God hears us, just as God heard the Israelites crying in Egypt. We hear the cries of our sisters and brothers next door and all around the world. God enters the lives of people, as Jesus entered Bartimaeus's life. Likewise, we are called to enter the struggle with one another, not because we are good, but because God is there in the struggle, there in the world, here in the world, already.

Sue Anne Steffey

The Stuff That Covenant Is Made Of

Genesis 18:9–15

The text of our sermon is part of a larger story, and I want to take a moment to fill in the familiar but all-important events in the history of Abraham and Sarah in a way that will give the human dynamics a fresh impact.

> Go from your country and your kindred and your father's house to the land that I will show you. And I will make of you a great nation, and I will bless you, and make your name great. (Gen. 12:1)

Abram, confident in God's covenant, a promise of land and posterity, responds in a way that fulfills all the images about him that loom large in our minds. The great patriarch, a citadel of faith and fear, rises up, takes Sarai, his wife, and Lot, his nephew, leaves Ur, his hometown, to travel to a land he doesn't know, but which he hopes might have milk and honey. After long hard days, weeks, months on the road, the travelers arrive at the land that Yahweh has promised them. Abram, tired but relieved, quickly builds an altar in gratitude to God; then looks up from the altar to see both that the land is inhabited by another people (no small issue this, it's the foundation of the Arab-Israeli conflict so present in our lives today), and not that only is there no milk and honey here, but famine in this land, bloated bellies and all that goes with starvation.

17

"Go from your country . . ."

In order to keep his little band from starvation, Abram leads them down into Egypt where food is available. When he is about to enter that country he says to Sarai, "I know you are a woman beautiful to behold, and when the Egyptians see you they will say, 'This is his wife, let's kill him and cash in on his goods.' Say you are my sister, that it may go well with me because of you, and that my life may be spared on your account." So, while at the Pharoah's palace Sarai is being known in the biblical sense of that word, Abram is getting fat on sheep and oxen with menservants and maidservants and camels. Now this setup doesn't please Yahweh much, so he sends great plagues on the Pharoah who soon discovers the cause, sends for Abram, evicts him from Egypt, and the little band winds up back where they had first pitched their tent. Like Alice in Wonderland they are running hard and getting nowhere fast. Abram looks less of a patriarch to you and me, but God's faith toward him is constant, and the covenant remains.

"Go from your country . . ."

This next section of the saga could be entitled Rescue the Relative from the Jam He's Gotten Himself Into. On their return from Egypt, Abram and Lot discover the land cannot support them together. Abram gives his nephew his choice of acreage. Lot, desiring green grass to grow under his feet, chooses the Jordan valley, well-watered like a garden, leaving Abram a rather arid piece of desert. The problem, you may recall, is that the inhabitants of the lush valley are wickedly greedy people who just happen to grab Lot and his possessions on their way to grabbing something else. Abram dutifully goes to rescue Lot from the grave that he has dug for himself. Another detour but the covenant remains.

"Go from your country . . ."

Now what of this covenant? As onlookers to the stage, you and I might comment—and rightly so—that it looks like a lot of promise and not much fulfillment. It's been twenty-four years since the covenant of land and offspring was first made, twenty-four years for the covenant of the land and posterity. Well, Abram is inhabiting the land—but in the original covenant there was no mention that the Kenites, the Kenizzites, the Kadmonites, the Hittites, the Perizzites, the Rephiam, the Amorites, the Canaanites, the Girgashites, and the Jebusites would be sharing the promised land with him. As for the covenant of posterity, Abram and Sarai are childless.

> And as if to add insult to injury, when Abram questions Yahweh on the subject, God answers, "Look toward the heavens and number the stars, so shall your descendants be."

> And as if to add insult to injury God goes on to tell Abram that those descendants will be sojourners in a land that is not their own and oppressed for four hundred years!

> And as if to add insult to injury God goes through the whole renaming bit—Abram to Abraham, Sarai to Sarah because God *has made* Abraham a father of a multitude of nations, and Abraham laughs because he and Sarah don't even have one son.

The covenant has not been broken but it rather reminds me of a flashing sign that says Free Car Wash with a Fill-up, and I drive in only to discover that the fill-up must be over fifteen gallons and my gas tank holds only ten. The covenant's not been broken, but it rather reminds me of my friend Bob, an executive for North American Rockwell. He'd come a long way: born in Harlem, he struggled his way through a slum school-system into City University of New York. He had a nice home in Queens, good wife, great kids, his life was moving swimmingly until through his church he started to visit the prisons on Saturdays. Within a period of time, he felt a covenant was being made—a promise of *satisfaction* and *blessing* and *grace* if he would leave the corporate land that he knew and go to seminary. But the voice didn't tell him his wife would leave him when the money stopped coming in, or of the alienation and loneliness he would feel from the younger students at the school, or how hard hitting the books would be when he was out of practice.

The covenant has not been broken but it reminds me of the girl who felt she should play little-league ball. She followed the voice of her covenant into the courts and onto the fields but the voice never told her the fact that she'd never really feel a part of the team; never told her about losing her girl friends who accused her of being different, of going into a strange land. The covenant has not been broken but it reminds me of the conflict of the promises we hear from this pulpit, and the everyday doldrums of dirty dishes, disappointment, and despair.

Despair is where we left Abraham, believing in the substance of the covenant but despairing of the details. For if his descendants were to number the stars, he didn't understand how; at ninety-nine he had given up hope of a son. But Abraham carries on, carries on until three visitors come toward his tent in the heat of the day. Abraham greets them with courteous and generous hospitality; slaughters a calf, rarely eaten in the East, and stands by the guests to see that they receive every attention necessary.

Then one of the guests, in disguise, begins to give Abraham some of the details of which he has despaired. In the spring Sarah will have a son. But the disclosure of the guest's divine identity does not come until . . . until Sarah laughs. She laughs in doubt, yes; my grandmother had the same reaction when I asked her last week "Do you realize Sarah was ten years older than you are when she had her first child?'' She giggles in doubt, but I wonder if Sarah laughs also at the irony of the event.

The irony? Yahweh's response to Sarah's laughter is, "Is there anything too hard for the Lord?'' It is the Hebrew word *niphal* "difficult, beyond human capacity"; but it has a second meaning: "strange, awkward, out of the ordinary.'' While Sarah is trying to integrate the difficulty of the task which, she well knows, Yahweh will accomplish, does she not laugh also at its strangeness, its awkwardness—pregnant when all her friends are sitting back to enjoy their golden years? Out of the ordinary, the stuff that covenant is made of.

So Sarah's laughter is faith's companion. Not merely heard at the beginning of salvation history, it remains audible and we hear it in our lives today. For each life of the covenant (Abraham's, Sarah's, yours, and mine) contains doubts and detours, fearful interruptions and disagreeable developments, high expectations and struggling hopes—the stuff that covenant is made of.

Karen L. Bloomquist

The Yes That Heals
Our Paralysis

We have all known people who are continually seeing the bad side of life. They are the pessimists who seem always to dwell on the negative. Their lives seem to be one big No! They complain about how terrible conditions are in their city and world. "No one is any good." They refuse to respond to their neighbor's need. Their negative attitude is often interrelated with physical sickness. When they are healed of their sickness, or when they are encountered with the affirming Yes of another person, they don't know how to respond. Yes indicates a life stance foreign to them. They may be healed of their sickness, or have their problem solved, but a more serious sickness remains. They are locked into being No persons. Their lives are still gigantic Noes.

A great number of people today have strains of such pessimism in them. It's as prevalent among Christians as among those who have no belief. It hits us when we feel we've "missed the mark," that we haven't lived up to God's expectations, our family's expectations, our own expectations. We are inflicted with it when we judge ourselves according to some outward standard and find ourselves lacking. Forces within and without tell us we're not OK—shout No to us. We become locked into the same trap when we brood over the past and actually covet what has been. We think of when our congregation was much bigger, and become depressed over the small remnant that remains. We covet those years when we were young and active, when the streets were safe to walk on at night, when we lived in a friendly small town.

The Hebrew people fell into doing the same thing. They remembered how God had acted in their history through the event of the Exodus, and when they were out on the desert or in exile in Babylon many years later, they longed for the "good old days." "Why can't God act as he did then?" they asked. But when in exile, removed from their homeland, they were in a state of paralysis. Into that situation, God's word comes through the prophet Isaiah:

> Remember not the former things,
>   nor consider the things of old.
> Behold, I am doing a new thing;
>   now it springs forth, do you not perceive it?
>   (Isa. 43:18–19a)

The people were so bound to their past that they were unable to respond to God in the present. Yet God was still active amid the dismal circumstances they found themselves in. God was continuing to say Yes to them, but all they could hear was No. "I will make a way in the wilderness and rivers in the desert" (Isa. 43:19b), said God—a loud Yes in the midst of their feelings of defeat and judgment.

Perhaps their problem and ours is that we have a distorted picture of who God is. If our mental image of God is that of a stern judge who is continually shaking "his" finger at us, we're not likely to feel very positive about ourselves or our situation. How else can we depict God? I propose that we try depicting God as having (1) a big heart, (2) an open ear, and (3) an outstretched arm. That's all! An accepting, forgiving, all-embracing God of love. A God who listens and reaches out to us, and to all people. A God who redemptively affirms us, in spite of what we have or have not done. A God who

breaks in with the unexpected, with a newness that overwhelms us and our past.

The God we meet in Scripture says Yes to us again and
again. As Paul writes, Jesus Christ is the Yes to our life—not
a No that is continually finding fault, but a Yes that affirms:
"For all the promises of God find their Yes in him" (2 Cor.
1:20). It's a Yes that we and the world need so desperately to
hear. We get so down on ourselves and the conditions in our
world that we don't hear God's Yes as it breaks through in
new ways—through new people, new forms, new vehicles.
As the church we haven't done very well in conveying God's
Yes to many people outside, who have instead heard us
saying No to people.

In the account of Jesus and the paralytic who was let down
through the roof (Mark 2:1-12), many think that the miracle
was Jesus' healing of the man's physical paralysis. They've
missed the point. Jesus is here dealing with a paralysis far
deeper and more serious than physical paralysis: a paralysis
of the total person. It is a paralysis of the spirit, and *that*
binds, entraps, and ensnares us into a state of being totally
immobilized. We are filled with a No that judges and overwhelms us with a feeling of defeat, of having failed God and
ourselves. Then the light breaks—the rivers arise in the
desert—God is made known in our midst, not with a No, but
with a Yes that truly heals our paralysis.

Notice Jesus' first words to the paralytic: " . . . your sins
are forgiven" (Mark 2:5), *not* "you are physically healed."
He doesn't even tell him to go cleanse himself! The words of
forgiveness do it all. They free up the man who had been in
such severe bondage of spirit, so that (of all things!) he is able
to rise and go home. What power those words of Jesus had
then, and what power they continue to have today when we
open ourselves up to allowing them to become the resounding Yes in our lives, the Yes that decisively frees us from

bondage to our past so that we can joyously live in response to God's activity in our present!

God's embracing acceptance is that which enables us to leave the bondage of rigidified traditions and oppressive sex roles, and to become whole people again. As a congregation, we are enabled not to brood over the past, but to be open to God's Yes in our present. God's Yes is shouted to us through new faces, new opportunities, new resources that open up for us.

With a big heart, an open ear, and an outstretched arm, God is present, transforming our pessimism. Listen and watch closely with the ears and eyes of faith to the resounding echoes of God's Yes in our own day.

Barbara B. Troxell

The No Which Enables
Our Yes

Exodus 3–4; Luke 1:26–56

Some years ago, in Santa Clara County, California, a family owned an orchard—one of many once filling this fertile valley—now sadly overrun by developers. The family had hundreds of acres of fruit trees, and employed numerous workers.

One day when the apricot crop was at its peak, additional help was needed. The owner asked his sons, who were learning the business, to go out into the orchard and help with the picking of apricots. The first son, when asked, said a quick and enthusiastic "Yes." Then he sat around, found more interesting things to do, and never went out of the office into the orchard.

The second son, when the father had earlier asked, said, flatly: "No, I won't go. It's awfully hot out there, and I'm no good at manual labor. I'd rather work on the books. No, father, I don't feel like picking cots."

Later, after thinking it over, realizing that bushels would be lost, and hearing inwardly the urgency of his father's request, the young man changed his mind, turned, went, and worked.

And Jesus said, "Which one did the will of the one who asked?" We know this story. In truth, it is ours.

A friend of mine who is leading groups in assertiveness training has given me a book she considers to be among the

26

best to emerge in this field: Herbert Fensterheim and Jean Baer, *Don't Say Yes When You Want to Say No* (New York: Dell Publishing, 1975).

Although I find myself questioning some aspects of the behavior-modification school of psychology, I am sparked by this title—for it resonates within my psyche; it speaks to my experience.

Very few personal commitments, decisions, choices are taken by simple, unequivocal acts of affirmation. Except for those rare individuals among us who perceive with such clarity that their words and actions are utterly congruent, most of us see many sides of an issue; envision various possibilities in a given situation; get hung on the horns of ambivalence; and when pushed hard, would in our heart of hearts rather, at first, say No than Yes.

Tonight I want to underscore the value of such tendencies; I want to cheer for the opposites within us; I want to affirm our No-saying—for I believe an early No to be a creative and ultimately enabling response.

Our texts this evening are very familiar: the calls of God to Moses and to Mary—significant figures in our sacred history, larger-than-life symbols of what it means for God *to speak* and *act* and *come alive* through human beings—through a young man and a young woman.

Each one is surprised by God, each one is well aware of his or her limitations, each one cannot quite believe God would choose him, her to lead in *this* way.

Look first with me at Moses. Five times he tries to squirm out of God's fiery grasp, to move away from under God's all-embracing presence. You heard his pleas, his questions, his begging-off. Listen to them now, as if they are ours—for they are:

"Who am I that I should go to Pharaoh, and bring the children of Israel out of Egypt?" (Who *me*, Lord? I'm just a plain ordinary shepherd . . . I'm just a rural pastor . . . *me*, go and challenge the government . . . the authorities . . . the oppressive power? You must have the wrong person, God . . .)

"And *who* shall I *say* told *me* to go to Egypt and do these things? What if the people ask me your name? *Who are you, anyway?*

(I need some authority other than myself. Who shall I say sent me to *leave* the flock committed to my charge and go to the place of power to protest? Who gave me permission to lead the people in this way? *What is your name?*)

"But if I tell them 'I AM WHO I AM' sent me—even if I tell them that it is the God of my fathers and mothers who sent me—they won't believe me, or listen to me." (They don't easily accept things like divine appearances, and the hearing of loud voices. What if they say I am mad, crazy, irrational? I'll lose their respect, and *then* where will that get us, God? I need to *prove* to them in some way that it really is You who want to speak through me and use *me* to lead the people.)

"Oh, my Lord, I am not eloquent, . . . but I am slow of speech, and of tongue. (I can't speak to that group, or to the powers-that-be; I'm OK among people I know, within a congregation where trust has built up between us; but preaching to those who don't even *know* me . . .? You're asking the impossible, Lord!)" And after God had responded to every one of Moses' cries, his attempts to get loose, finally, Moses in desperation, frustration, utter fear pleads with God:
"Oh, my Lord, send, please send—I pray—somebody else!"
All these ways you and I have known in our own hearts.

And tonight I say to you and to myself—*we* are better off, and God is better off, if we *set forth our fears,* our *frustrations,* our *desperate pleas* for release from such responsibility. For if we do not get them out, they will nag and drag and hassle us all our life long—and render us virtually ineffectual and powerless.

Moses said what he felt. Moses bared his soul before God. And then he went—back to his father-in-law, Jethro, to be released from his shepherding of the flock and then off with his wife and children to Egypt—with his brother Aaron's help, to do the liberating will of God. Moses' Yes—Moses' leadership as a chosen one of God—was enabled by the freedom he felt from the beginning to say No in all sorts of forms.

A few thousand years later, a young maiden sits spinning, preparing the scarlet yarn for the weaving of the veil of the temple. This is her main task in life at the moment, according to one noncanonical source. She sits in virginal innocence, carefully working at spinning some yarn.

An angel, a messenger of God, comes to her, greeting her with great reverence and respect. *She is troubled at the saying*—for it is at the moment farthest from her mind that an angel would come to her with direct greetings from the Holy God. Gabriel tries to calm her and then to bring her the message that she will conceive and bear a son—in fact, the Son of the Most High.

Now, she *is* concerned . . . and raises the obvious question—

"How shall this be, seeing I know not a man?"

One of my favorite depictions of this scene is a Russian icon which has Mary, clothed in a brown, earth-color cloak, holding in her left hand a ball of scarlet yarn; her right hand upraised to guide thread from spindle. Gabriel, to our left in the icon, is coming towards Mary, his right arm outstretched.

We are drawn to their hands—Mary's pulling back in

surprise, in fright, in wonder; Gabriel's moving forward to make contact, to bless, to calm, to assure.

Their eyes do not connect with each other's, but are raised, as if to look together at a third point—to that Holy One who has brought them together.

Only after this moment of troubled surprise; only after raising a question; only after moving a hand in fearful wonder; only after being assured that her kinswoman, Elizabeth, is also in a similar place—*only then* does Mary say her Yes. *Fiat.*

"Let it be to me according to your word."
Then can she sing . . . "Tell out, my soul, the greatness of God!"

Moses and Mary experience what Kierkegaard somewhere has called "the alarming possibility of being able."

Both Moses and Mary test the voices, question the messenger, express their feelings, have the encouragement of another human being; then commitment, intentionality, determination, praise!

Both good Jews, Mary and Moses knew well how to interact directly with the One who created them, and who entered into covenant with them and their people.

When you and I look beyond Moses and Mary to Jesus, Supreme Son of the covenant, what do we discover? Near to the close of his earthly human life, we find Jesus in a desolate, darkening olive grove, with disciples asleep from worry, weariness, and fear, speaking an anguished prayer:

Abba, my Abba, if it be possible, remove this cup from me.
. . . Nevertheless, not my will, but thine, be done.

Note well what Jesus does *not* say: "Anything you want, God. I am nothing, your will is all-important. My feelings and fears, wants and desires don't count for anything. I know that. So do anything with me you want.'' How would Jesus' impact upon us and the world be different if this had been his prayer in Gethsemane—if he had simply prayed, "not my will, but thine, be done. . . ." (*without* the anguished prelude, "if it be possible")?

Jesus spoke his own No—his own desire for, perhaps, more time with his disciples, continuing opportunities with people, deeper understanding of his mission by others . . .

> Abba, dear Abba—dear Father God—if it be possible, remove this cup from me. . . .

Only then, having voiced where he is in the depths of his soul, does Jesus also cry out his obedience to God's will working through him:

> *Nevertheless, not my will, but thine, be done.*

The Christ-life, the transformation in Jesus spoken then, enabled him to face the excruciating cross; to embrace the darkness; to give up his life for God's sake and ours.

To trustful obedience, to covenant servanthood you and I are called, you and I—sons and daughters of Moses and Mary, brothers and sisters of Jesus. Trustful obedience is always born of the covenant relationship in which we have heard God's Yes to us, and can then voice to God the No of our ambivalence; the No of our fears and alarms; the No of our desires for self-preservation. And in our speaking of the No, we, with Moses and Mary and Jesus, hear *God's* No to us . . . which is part of God's great Yes:

> "No, I will not give you up, O child of mine. No, I will not let you go back to your old comfortable ways—to values and tasks which once were right for you; to your sheep-tending and your spinning, your flock-leading and your weaving; to the old familiar style—I want you for something more.

"I hear your No and I want you to hear mine, too. You have freedom at this point, and so do I—to keep on calling you, to keep on with our covenant, to keep on drawing you to ever new creations which are to be born in and through you."

To what No is God calling you and me?

Is it No to a way of functioning which worked last year but will no longer?

Is it No to a good *past* collection of sermons and lectures which have lost their vitality?

Is it No to a once-creative style of ministry which is no longer viable?

Is it No to a *level of consuming* which we have begun to see that our bodies and our earth cannot bear?

Is it No to an *economic order* which leads to enormous salary differences, having nothing to do with *need*?

Is it No to all that perhaps was once life-giving but is now death-dealing inwardly and outwardly, individually and corporately?

When you and I get in touch with these, then truly we can sing with Mary that ancient song of her people:

God has scattered the proud in the imagination of their hearts,
God has put down the mighty from their thrones,
and exalted those of low degree;
God has filled the hungry with good things, and the rich he has sent empty away.

Such was the promise to our ancestors and to their children.

Elie Wiesel, contemporary Jewish author and teacher, survivor as a youth of a death camp where he watched his father die an agonizing death of cold and starvation—tells us in story after story of the eternal dialogue of Yes and No between his people and God . . . the God who was with them in all the places of their suffering, yet the God whom they felt again and again had forsaken them and had to be called back, be brought to account. Listen to one such tale—inscribed on the end page of Wiesel's *Town Beyond the Wall.*

> Legend tells us that one day [Humanity] spoke to God in this wise:
> "Let us change about. You be Humanity, and I will be God. For only one second."
> God smiled gently and asked Humanity, "Aren't you afraid?"
> "No. And you?"
> "Yes, I am," God said.
> Nevertheless God granted Humanity's desire. God became human, and Humanity took God's place and immediately availed themselves of God's omnipotence: Humanity refused to revert to their previous state. So neither God nor [Humanity was ever the same again].
> Years passed, centuries, perhaps eternities. And suddenly the drama quickened. The past for one, and the present for the other, were too heavy to be borne.
> As the liberation of the one was bound to the liberation of the other, they renewed the ancient dialogue whose echoes come to us in the night, charged with hatred, with remorse, and most of all, with infinite yearning.*

To the renewal of this ancient dialogue, in whatever form is appropriate and needful for each of us and for God in our time, I call us this night: to the dialogue of the covenant relationship wherein we are free to say our Noes, to voice our quarrels with God, to speak out our surprise and amazement and fear, AND to be attentive to *God's* fear, *God's* wonder, God's Yes and No to us. "Don't Say Yes When You Want to Say No." Our Yes is stronger when our No is honored. God's Yes to us and in us is stronger when God's

---

*Elie Wiesel, *Town Beyond the Wall,* trans. S. Becker (New York: Holt, Rinehart & Winston, 1964). Copyright © 1964 by Elie Wiesel. Used by permission.

No is honored in our lives. The necessity, not just the option, of creative Nay-saying is laid upon you and me. *No*—not as damper or depressant, not as cop-out or as compromise but just the opposite—*No* as affirmation of others, of self, of the earth, of life, of God.

When we have learned to say No, and to receive the No of God, we can receive and act on the Yes which is in every No—No—No—No of life.

The struggle and dialogue of the two brothers, to respond to the one who calls, continues within us.

Valerie Russell

Giving Thanks or Making Do

Genesis 32:22–31; Mark 12:28–34

THANKSGIVING

One of today's popular folk songs comes from a familiar piece of Scripture: "To everything there is a season—turn, turn, turn." Well, here we are at Thanksgiving which marks the beginning, in some ways, of the season of seasons! We are called to come together as a people to count our blessings. I must confess in my own experience I have most often thought that meant "packing up our sorrows" and fears and "putting on a happy face," which wasn't *always* reflective of my feelings inside. We are often admonished to "stiffen the old upper lip," to "be a rock in a time of uncertainty and disease," and to remember that after all there is much for which we should be eternally grateful.

Now I would be the last person (accused of being one of the great idealists!) to deny the authenticity or the necessity of shouting out our blessing or of looking towards the bright side of things. *It is always important for us to place our lives in the context of the big picture.* Such awareness of the juxtaposition of our gifts is one of the ways we survive. And I also believe that unmitigated joy is one of the things we Christians have the hardest time celebrating!

Unfortunately, we too often end up celebrating platitudes. There is a cartoon of Ziggy looking at a poster which says: "If you always look down you'll miss the sunshine," to which Ziggy responds: "Yes, but you won't fall into any big hole, either!"

Perhaps one reason we have difficulty with authentic celebration is that underneath that kind of thankfulness lurks the reality of our existential situations—not just the happy things but the collage of our stories. I got to thinking about this while reading today's assigned Scripture from the New Testament, a passage which can stand as our challenged response as children of God. "You shall love the Lord your God with all your heart and with all your soul and with all your mind and with all your strength, and your neighbor as yourself." That is quite a specific response. Jesus was so specific about it, you will remember, that "no one dared to ask him any questions."

A few weeks ago, I was watching "Mary Hartman, Mary Hartman." She uttered, "Lately I feel like every play is a third-down play." Abruptly my psyche yelled "Ouch" to my mind!

Three weeks ago I lost a close friend who died of cancer. Bob Moss was also President of the United Church of Christ. He was a good and faithful human being. We had been on many important exhilarating adventures together. He was one of those persons beside whom you felt you could change the world and do it humanly. And as I tried to wrestle with what it meant to *stand beside him* as he struggled with death, I couldn't get the question out of mind: How do we give thanks when we live in a world of people and nations where we feel everyday that so much is at stake? The *tenuousness* of our earthly journey clamors that we are always in third-down situations where the results can bounce either way.

I attended the United Church of Christ's Pacific and Asian American Ministries Conference last summer. We were asked in faith exploration groups to sum up the Bible, renaming it in five books in modern parlance. One man in my group said he could rename the bulk of the Old Testament: *Making Do in the Promised Land.*

As I thought about that, it became clear to me that we can, we must give thanks for our *survival,* but "making-do theology" is hardly the response of loving or praising with our *whole* minds, or our *whole* strength. Celebrating our ability to make do and survive is a piece of our call to thankfulness, but not the whole story. So, friends, this morning I'd like to share some of the ingredients as I see them before us—to teach us the lessons, and to open our hearts and lives to deeper and more real conditions of thankfulness and response.

The first ingredient to me is to reexamine our *definition* of caring. A priori to loving God—ourself, our neighbor—is at least the ability to "give a damn."

Henri Nouwen, in a sermon originally preached here a few years ago, defined the word *care* this way, "the root of the word 'care' comes from *kara* which means to lament. The basic meaning of *care* is to grieve, to experience sorrow, to cry out with. He went on to point out that, "this definition is very difficult to accept for those of us who tend to look at caring as an attitude of the *strong* toward the *weak,* of the *powerful* toward the *powerless,* of the *haves* toward the *have-nots.*" In fact we feel quite uncomfortable with an invitation to enter into the pain of someone else *before* attempting to do something about it! We haven't learned Dan Berrigan's admonition: "Don't just do something—Stand There!"

Yet when we ask ourselves who means the most in our lives we often find it's those who, before offering cures or solutions, are *first* the ones who have chosen to share our pain and "touch our wounds with a gentle and a tender hand."

This is critical because at Thanksgiving we're often

prompted to enter shallow forms of caring for the "least fortunate." We are asked to share our food, but not our love, nor our presence. The gospel imperative certainly calls us not only to be our brothers' and sisters' keeper but primarily our brothers' and sisters' *brother and sister*. To be indifferent to that kind of caring is to be indifferent toward life's ambiguities and toward the mutual needs and gifts of every relationship. To *care* with all our hearts, our minds, our souls *is to be present* to those ambiguities within the context of the knowledge of our common vulnerability.

The second ingredient is a deeper thankfulness which builds on the first. For me it is dramatically embodied in the story of Jacob wrestling with the angel until the break of dawn. With an awareness of ambiguity and vulnerability this story dramatically highlights the great act of risk. Imagine the scene: A man, sitting in the middle of nowhere, in pitch-darkness, left alone, wrestling with some unknown force (God, an angel, the devil???) Robert Reiner dramatizes the moment when he says, "Do you know what it is to be mugged by some awful power in the night?" I do. Jacob is wrestling with the gray areas of life—not sure whether it is angel or demon he struggles with, he walks nonetheless boldly into the area of possible transformation. There is found the hope. We are called to believe that taking hold will make the difference.

I have found that the only way to deal with the grief of the loss of anything vital to us is to walk into the terror and pain, praying for some unimaginable blessing. Here the Christian credibility card is called for because we must distinguish between optimism (assessing the odds) and hope (looking for things unseen).

My friend, Jim Dittes of Yale Divinity School, once wrote me, "Most of us must learn about trusting and fearing before we can learn about living with healing grace."

Jacob in his lonely and solitary struggle, in ultimate desperation to recover meaning and reconciliation, seeks out of that powerlessness the ultimate empowerment, a blessing—how to live and be touched with healing grace. He is lamed by the experience—forever after he has a new walk and a new name.

Thus, for me this Thanksgiving, one of the ingredients called for from us is that we stand out in the ambiguous dark, not attempting to be God or even like God, but coming as ourselves with aching and longing, looking for some disclosure of God and finding it within us. A wise man once said, "The single most important thing we need to learn in order to discover God, is how to let God be 'God in us!' "

The act of caring is the act of tenderness. The act of wrestling through the night with some unknown force is the act of boldness. They are part of the same spectrum when it comes to fulfilling the great commandment and they are both forms which bring the bearers of grace!

Third, lest we see the challenges of caring and boldness only in personalistic or individualistic terms, this Thanksgiving we are called to reflect on who we are *corporately*: as a nation and as a church. As a nation and church we have exploited people everywhere. In the name of democracy and of Jesus Christ we have handed people the artifacts of our faith and ideals and taken from them their land. We have stood in doorways denying equal education to little black boys and girls as we recite our "Hail Mary full of grace" and "Our Father who art in heaven . . . forgive us our trespasses." And we have built and perpetuated a theology based on patriarchal tradition and the fact that "after all, Jesus was a man," and this has shaped attitudes and behavior which too often excludes half the human family.

One response called for from us this Thanksgiving is to stand present to life's ambiguities, not bewailing our guilt, but through caring and boldness acknowledging the implicit wholeness of God's world.

Perhaps to love our neighbors as ourselves means simply *to use what we've got* as a way of sharing the reality of our oneness. But if we are not going to be caught by the power syndrome in our sharing (the haves vs. the have-nots), we have to move back to one thankful affirmation that we have, all of us, been loved by God.

While in India I met a priest who said to us one day, "If we did not believe in Jesus Christ as we sit here today, you Americans would be the parent and I would be the child, but because we all believe in Jesus, we can sit here as brothers and sisters."

Perhaps it is our corporate wrestling to become new people which is most threatening. For it may mean emptying ourselves, moving back to the ground of our vulnerability before we can respond faithfully to the sharing of what we have and what we are with the world and the world with us. *The only thing worse than being perceived as the victim is being perceived as the enemy!* The whole concept of building global interdependence involves breaking down those simplistic, though perhaps historically accurate, perceptions by becoming new people.

Perhaps it is best put by the story of the Zen master and professor. The professor went to understand Zen and the Zen master served her tea. He filled the professor's cup and kept pouring until it overflowed. The professor finally shouted, "It is overfull—no more will go in!" "Like the cup," said the Zen master, "you are full of your own opinions and speculations. How can you learn unless you first empty your cup?"

I guess what I'm trying to say is that it is important to give thanks for the content of our blessings. They are the tools and the people by and with whom we survive. They describe for us the quality of our very selves. They help us cope in this work, and coping is something to be thankful for. Making do in the promised land *is* beautiful.

Yet somehow, the deeper magic, the grace and power, in our giving thanks is related to our approach to the unknowns:

—to learning how to stand even tentatively in care and solidarity beside each other with no answers, with no more than clues

—to learning through boldness to wrestle with unknowns, trying to find God in the midst of them

—to daring to approach the kind of power which enables us to empty our full cups in a way that means we will be newly filled and our past arrogances will be corrected.

In each of these ambiguous moments God often comes to us with amazing healing. Therefore, we approach this Thanksgiving not as people *who have arrived,* but as men and women on a journey towards possibilities which even now we see only dimly. As in all liberation struggles, this Thanksgiving we celebrate the already and the not-yet.

I wish for us all the caring, boldness, and power that will make us new.

Happy Thanksgiving

Monika K. Hellwig

The Expectation and
the Birth

THE FOURTH SUNDAY IN ADVENT

Christmas, to most of us, spells joy but also unfulfilled longing. It is a time to remember what has been, and also what
has not been—a time to acknowledge the pain of unfulfilled
promises. This is Christmas for each of us and Christmas for
the Christian community. Yet the pain of Christmas is not
the pain of despair, but that of hope.

This time of Advent has been one of expectation—but
expectation of what? Quite concretely, we have been buying
(perhaps even making) presents for family and friends; we
have been teaching our children Christmas carols, perhaps
preparing a play or pageant; we have been baking cakes and
cookies and preparing a season of celebration; we are ready
to trim the tree and set out the Nativity scene, passing on in
story and image and song the vision and the mystery of the
wonderful birth among us. If we are particularly devout, we
may have marked the observance of the weeks of Advent
with Bible readings, the construction of a Jesse tree, the
lighting of candles on an Advent wreath. We may have done
all these things, attempting to counteract in our homes the
commercial aspects of Christmas that threaten to crowd out
its spiritual meaning. We may have done these things as a
way of learning to pray and of giving our children an opportunity to learn to pray.

However, Christmas means more than passive expectation, quiet recollection of the wonderful intervention of God in our world and our history in times past, a moment of turning to God in prayer. If the Salvation Army and others have brought it to our attention, we may have remembered that Christmas is also the time to think of the dispossessed and the forgotten. Perhaps we have sent a check to some overseas relief fund, donated clothes to a local collection, or packed a Christmas basket for a needy family.

But all these responses honor an order of things already established. If they spell expectation, then it is the expectation of sameness, of repetition, of the cycles of the seasons, and the lives of human persons. If they speak of a birth, it seems to be a birth like any other, though more universally remembered.

How different are the thoughts proposed to us in the Advent Bible-readings of the churches. Though varying slightly in their selections, the readings for Lutheran, Roman Catholic, Episcopal, and Presbyterian services at this time have powerful common themes. Visionary dreams of the prophets direct our gaze toward a distant horizon of promise. Colorful Gospel stories turn our attention to the birth of Jesus in time, in the past. The letters of the apostles urge us to reflect on the way we are living our Christian lives in the present, poised as we are between the future of the divine promise and the past of the divine initiative.

The future of the prophetic promises is a future of radical transformation: wolves and lambs are to lie down together in trusting safety; deserts are to bloom and yield a ready livelihood; the blind are to see and the deaf to hear; captives shall go home in joy; there shall be plenty for the poor; and the nations shall worship together in peace on the mountain of the Lord. It is all too easy to let these readings float by us like a happy fairy-tale dream of things that can never really be. It may also be easy to assume that this must simply be taken to refer to some spiritual fulfillment in the inner space of individual consciousness or in the outer space of a spirit-life beyond death and time. Yet serious reflection on the Hebrew Scriptures and on the teachings of Jesus taken in their own context does not seem to allow such an interpretation. It seems rather to demand an interpretation of the prophets' visionary dreams in terms of a radical transformation of the conditions of human life and community within the public sphere of history in which our lives are shaped and lived. The mode of expression is poetic and highly imaginative, but the intent is not only serious but quite sober. The promises are interspersed with threats of terrible doom to follow if the promises are not realized. The meaning is: the stakes are high and our concern is for a destiny that is our common destiny, in which there can be no by-passing of the issues.

Because the language of the prophets is poetic, we are left with a task of practical interpretation. It might be thought that the other Scripture readings fill the gap, but they turn out to be poetic and mysterious too. The Gospel stories, in fact, tell of classic encounters and situations. Facts are certainly related there, but far more important than the facts are the comments on our human situation and God's judgment upon it. It is in living the Christian reality in our own lives that we come to see in sharper focus the judgment that God makes on the way we run the world and relate to one another. This may be why dedicated Christians throughout the centuries have come to identify more and more with the poor and the outcast, bringing to the fore in the birth stories the aspects of rejection, poverty, and oppression.

Certainly, one can look at the stable scene in two ways. On the one hand there is the romantic scene of simplicity, wonder, intimacy, the song of angels, the joy of parents and shepherds, the gifts of the Magi—wisdom, pomp, and power dissolved momentarily in contemplation and celebration. On the other hand, there are the poor, taxed beyond endurance, required to make a preposterous mid-winter journey from Galilee into the bitter, cold winds of the Judean wilderness, with no consideration for the hardships of such a trip with a baby due any day and no possible way of finding shelter among the large crowds. Then there is the response of Herod: If there is a spark of royal promise among the poor and dispossessed, a hope for the future among the crushed and the outcast, all potential bearers of such hope must be slaughtered for not knowing "their place" in the permanent scheme of things— for "their place" is below the properly human, to provide a platform on which the achievements of the privileged may be built.

The Gospels tell us that when the word of God is spoken into history it is spoken in the person of the utterly powerless and oppressed—a word that reveals the outrage of the situation. The person who is uniquely the image of God, is by human evaluation classed with the "less than human"—with all those less than human who are also, of course, the image of God, and who are called to stand upright on the earth and share in creating a future in hope.

Again, at this juncture, it would be all too easy to let our Scripture readings slip by, with a passing note on the merciful compassion of God who is willing to intervene in history even on these terms. It would also be easy and tempting to profess shocked disbelief for what happened at that distant place so long ago. However, certain of our readings "call our bluff." The apostle's searching inquiry into the way we live—as Christians between the past of the Gospel stories and the ultimate future of the promised reign of God— questions our sincerity. To give to the overseas relief funds, to the clothing collections, to the food baskets is not a problem as long as the poor and the excluded "know their

place" in our world, and do not attempt any radical change in
the social and economic order which would put them in
competition with us for the privileges and benefits to which
we have laid exclusive claim. *We* see no problem as long as
they see no future for themselves.

The question that Advent and Christmas pose to us is
above all the question of God who confronts us in the person
of the poor—the question about the radical newness of the
future we are willing to meet (and even to make). It is a
question about the quality of our expectation, and of our
understanding of the meaning of this birth.

M. Nadine Foley, O. P.

A Homily for Midnight Mass

Isaiah 9:1–6; Titus 2:11–14; Luke 2:1–14

CHRISTMAS

The word of God incarnate in Jesus Christ, whose birth into our human history we celebrate tonight, addresses the enduring paradox of our human existence. This paradox has been expressed in numerous ways, but particularly well, I think, in an eighteenth-century rabbinic tale of a worshipper, Ben Ezra, who, on the eve of Yom Kippur prayed long and ardently in the synagogue, much to the distress of the waiting rabbi. His impatience overcome by his curiosity, the rabbi at length inquired of his zealous worshipper, "Ben Ezra, what is it that you say to the Master, that it takes you so long?"

"I will tell you what I have been saying," said Ben Ezra. "To the Master of the Universe I say, 'These are my sins and I confess them:

> I argued with my wife. But you know my wife.
> I lost patience with my children. But what parent doesn't?
> I cheated a little in the shop. But just a little. Among friends.
> How small my sins are, Master of the Universe!
> Now consider your sins.
> You dry up the sky, and our crops wither.
> Other times they burn up because you send too much sun.
> You let the rains come before the poor man has the roof repaired.

47

You do not stop war, and young men die.
The marriage bed is empty; there is no child in the womb.
You take away the light from the eyes of a child, and he is
    blind.
You take away our loved ones, and we are left alone until
    we die.
These are your sins, Master of the Universe, and they are
    very great.
But I will make you a proposition:
You forgive me my little sins, and I will forgive you your
    great ones!'

That was my proposal, Rabbi, and I ask you, was that so
wrong?'' The rabbi did not answer for a long time.''No, Ben
Ezra,'' he said at last, ''it was not wrong; it was not wrong.
But why, but why did you drive so small a bargain? For sins
like these you could have asked him to send the Messiah.
You could have asked him to redeem the world.''

In the wisdom of the rabbi the afflictions of human persons
are so incomprehensible and so persistent that nothing other
than God himself, in his saving presence, could adequately
address them. We believe this too. It is precisely because we
believe it that we gather tonight at this midnight hour, when
all things are in quiet silence,

    in a shared faith, different from that of Ben Ezra and
    his rabbi,
    and a common experience—
A *shared faith,* because we assent, in varying degrees and
with differing insights,

    to the wonder of the Incarnation
    to the mystery breaking into human history
        in the birth of the child, Jesus Christ, 2000 years ago;
    and while we will never fully understand, *we believe.*

A common experience, because Christmas speaks to us
   of warmth and love
   of generosity and sacrifice
   of friendship and family
   of laughter and play and joy.
   It arouses memories of when we were more
   childlike than now,
            when we would allow the play of imagination
                                        and fancy,
            when we were more carefree
                     more protected
                     more loved perhaps.
            And we yearn to recapture those times.
            That yearning may be the deepest longing
                                of our hearts.
So once again, with our strange human mixture of *faith* and
feelings, we come together as we have done in the past
   to hear the familiar carols
   to sense the presence of friends
   to savor the words of prophecy and fulfillment,
      the message of a Savior born in the fullness of time and
      of a redemption assured.
   Once more tonight, as so frequently during Advent, we
heard the prophet Isaiah speak of the coming of the Prince of
Peace who would once and forever secure for us a reign of
justice and peace. We heard again Luke's account of the
birth of Jesus in Bethlehem where angels appeared to lowly
shepherds, singing a message of glory to God and of peace to
people such as ourselves. Is it not strange that thoughts such
as these should occupy our minds?
   Yet are we not a bit deluded to be talking of ancient
prophets with promises of salvation; of angels speaking
strange messages to illiterate peasants; of stars in the

heavens guiding foreign potentates across alien deserts to the village of Bethlehem? Even more to the point, how can we talk of a reign of justice and peace when, after almost 2000 years of faith experience,

wars are still waged

people starve in ever greater numbers

nations of believing people work oppression and injustice upon others

and the very earth groans under the burden of human habitation?

Ought we not rather to be beseeching the Father for the Messiah in the manner of Ben Ezra and his rabbi? The incongruity of it all is not lost upon skeptics and unbelievers, and they are quick to point it out.

Surely, too, there are times when we who call ourselves Christian are struck with the paradox of our faith.

For we are Christians of our own age.

We are, after all, people to whom feats of space exploration are commonplace. Do we not know how to navigate by means of stars?

Achievements of modern communication are so extraordinary as to be almost miraculous. What need have we of angels?

Travel from country to country is accomplished with the speed of sound. So what is so extraordinary about kings crossing deserts?

What, then, is to be said of this faith of ours, by which we hold that *an apparently obscure event of the birth of a child almost two centuries ago is a central point in a redemptive history in which we continue to live today?*

The birth of Jesus Christ is no ordinary event in the recorded history of peoples. Ordinary historic events are marked down, remembered, and possibly commemorated year after year. In time a given occurrence may fade into insignificance as others capture the imagination. But the birth, life, and death of Jesus Christ does not belong to this kind of history. Once born, once having lived through the Pascal mysteries of death and resurrection, Jesus Christ is an ever present reality; in him we live and breathe and have our being even now. This is our faith. To say this and to believe this, is to say something different about time and the manner of our participation in it. Human history is measured by dates on a time line that mark the deeds, events, and lives of great persons, nations, and peoples. This is *historic time. We live in it.*

It is the time of human achievements, discoveries, explorations, settlements, scientific and technological advances, the production of artistic masterpieces, as well as the time of wars, pestilences, and famine.

Redemptive history is something else. It is not measured at all.

It is a continuum of events in which God has acted for our salvation. Some call it *mythic time.*

It encompasses and envelops and moves through our human history, but it is not contained by it.

By our faith and sacramental life we are caught up in it. *It lives in us.*

The event of our Savior's birth is a definitive point of convergence between historic and redemptive time, not the first, nor certainly the most significant, but a most emphatic one. The promise communicated by God in ages past and spoken by the prophets in his name is fulfilled. The Word spoken by God is incarnated and manifested as Emmanuel, God with us. When we commemorate this event this night, we do not merely remember it, we enter into it.

Truly the Word was made flesh and *dwelt* among us as John tells us.

But the Word made flesh *dwells* among us even now, as we know in faith.

And as, in our celebration, we are caught up in the dimension of redemptive time, we know with certainty
that our salvation is assured
that peace of mind and heart is a reality
that justice is established
that the poor, the hungry, and the afflicted are loved and cared for.

And all of this, despite the fact that in the dimension of historic time we are certain only that none of this is assured.
The world lies unredeemed in its peoples and in all parts of our earth.
Our penance rite tonight calls that fact dramatically to our attention; as does the prayer of Ben Ezra.

Possibility and hope for our world lie in the fact that redemptive time and historic time meet in the Savior who is born this night; and in the fact that they meet also in us who are incorporated into him through our sacramental life. And that for us is the point worth pondering and pondering again. Christians, you and I, are called to live in the tension point where historic and redemptive time converge.

We are called to know the joy, the peace, the hope, the love that Christ infallibly confers upon those who join themselves to him. We are called not only to know his joy, his peace, his hope, and his love for ourselves, but to be bearers of these redemptive gifts into the lives of others. We are called to participate in the anguish, the pain, the deprivation, and the suffering of those around us. And we are called to minister to our world—to bring the certainty of our hope, known by us in redemptive time, into active work to better the circumstances of contemporary people so many of whom are doomed to suffering. In short, we are called to mediate the reality of the salvation which we experience in redemptive time into the unsaved, unredeemed, corrupted world of which we are a part.

We can fail in our calling, and we have, because our temptation is to move out of the tension point. We can retreat into the comfort of our faith, withdrawing into a kind of self-centered preoccupation with God, concerned only with personal sin and personal salvation. Or we can forsake the faith dimension of our lives, plunging frantically into social action programs for the benefit of others, fashioning salvation according to our own designs. But either is to miss the point of Emmanuel, God with us.

Let us use tonight's celebration of our Savior's birth to renew our faith; to reaffirm the truths that give meaning and purpose to our lives; and to rejoice that because we dwell in two reaches of time *we can always be more than we are,* for ourselves and for others.

This, in the end, is what the coming of Christ means for us. Ben Ezra and his rabbi could only be sad for they had not the same assurance of salvation that is ours in certainty. But for our part:

Let us be joyful.

Let us be full of hope.

Let us gift others with signs of our love.

Let us know peace in our hearts even though there be cause for anxiety.

And let us speak openly of shepherds and angels and wise men.

For God acts as he will, and we will never fully understand. Let us thank the Lord for this strange faith.

We live with Christ, caught up in the paradox of Incarnation, and we give glory to God who has made it so.

Cynthia Wedel

The Story of the Transfiguration

Matthew 17:1–9

EPIPHANY

This is the Sunday before Lent. In the Prayer Book it has
been called Quinquagesima—the fiftieth day before Easter.
It is a time when it seems appropriate to think about Lent,
and the use we might make of it for enriching or strengthen-
ing our lives as Christians. A traditional way of doing this
used to be "giving things up" for Lent. Perhaps all of us have
at some time given up candy or desserts or smoking or
drinking. And this certainly did us no harm—indeed, the
physical good may have been at least as real as the spiritual
benefit.

In recent years there has been more emphasis on doing
something extra in Lent—perhaps going to church more
often, or attending Lenten study classes, or following a plan
of private prayer or Bible reading. Again, since few of us
would probably claim to be overactive church members,
there is real merit in this.

However, I suspect that for many of us these outward
activities or observances have only slight value. The real
problem of faith for most of us is in our rather hazy knowledge of what the Christian church really teaches about God
and Jesus Christ, and our human understanding of and response to them. One aspect of Christian belief which comes
sharply to the foreground in Lent, Good Friday, and Easter

is the church's insistence—in the creeds and in all orthodox Christian teaching—on the divinity of Christ. The story of the transfiguration, which was the lesson today, is related to this teaching.

Most human beings through all of history have believed in powers, or the gods, or God as a force outside the universe which influences our lives and destinies. Real atheists are very hard to find because it is extremely difficult to believe that all the wonder and beauty and order of the universe could have happened by mere chance. We live in an era of questioning, doubt, and skepticism. Yet surveys and statistics indicate that most modern people still believe in a God of some kind—at least as a creative and moral force within the universe.

An interesting phenomenon of recent years has been the growth of the Jesus movement. Young people, and many of their elders, have been caught anew by the beauty, simplicity, strength, and love which shines forth in the Gospel accounts of Jesus. He is seen as a friend, companion, example, and teacher. His followers try to model their lives on his—to live simply, to show love to others, and to win them to a belief in and relationship with Jesus. It is the human Jesus they speak of. If asked about the traditional Christian emphasis on the divinity of Jesus, they frequently brush such questions aside as irrelevant. Their attitude seems to be, "Why confuse something as simple and beautiful as the story of Jesus with abstract theological questions?"

As you are probably aware, this is nothing new. Many of the Jews of Jesus' time and since have accepted him as a great example, teacher, prophet. Mohammed acknowledged him as a prophet in the line of Abraham, Moses, and Isaiah. It was the early church, following the teachings of Paul, which insisted stubbornly on the divinity of Christ—on the fact that he was in some mysterious way God *and* Man. In our day, Unitarians and Universalists do not accept Jesus as divine, though they read the Bible and accept his teachings. Indeed, if you know members of these churches you may discover that in terms of involvement in works of mercy and justice for all humankind they are often more active and concerned than those who belong to the more orthodox Christian churches.

What then can we think or say about our church's insistence on the fact that in Jesus Christ, the Almighty Creator of heaven and earth took on human form and lived among us as a humble carpenter? Does it really matter, as long as we try to be his disciples and follow his teachings?

I would like to share with you one of my husband's "parables" which I have found of great help in understanding this teaching of the church. First, we need to remember that the word *gospel* means "good news." The early church was able to win the world of its time with the good news which it preached. If it had been merely the news that a wonderful man had lived, taught, and died, and that if we would be as good and loving and brave as he was the world would be saved—would that really be good news? Human beings have always known they ought to be good and loving, but we always find it very difficult. It is easy to draw up moral codes. But where do we find the power and motivation to live up to them?

My husband called his parable "The Two Biographies of Jesus." The popular life of Christ is like a log-cabin-to-White-House story. A man, born in very humble circumstances, poor and unknown, begins through his teaching and preaching to draw others to follow him. For three years he moves through Palestine, telling stories, answering questions, healing people, and demonstrating great love and concern for the poor and oppressed. While the simple people responded, followed, and loved him, the authorities became very anxious lest he stir up a revolution or try to overthrow the government. Finally, the authorities plotted against him and had him arrested and executed on a trumped-up charge. But his life had been so beautiful that it has been remembered and honored all over the world for 2000 years. Surely no man in history has ever had such influence. He far outshines other heroes who have been born in humble circumstances, lived great lives, and died a martyr's death.

But that is not the story as the Bible records it and as the church recounts it. If we could call that the log-cabin-to-White-House story, the biblical version is the exact opposite. It is a White-House-to-log-cabin story—a totally improbable thing. Since the White House may have too many political overtones, let's shift the scene to England, back in the early Middle Ages, when the king still had the power of life and death over the people (as God has such power over us). People obeyed the king out of fear of his power, as human beings often obey God, or the gods, out of fear.

Then one day, the king disappeared from the palace. No one knew where he was, but he had left word that he would be back and had left trusted regents in charge of the kingdom. He was gone for three years.

During that time he lived, entirely incognito, in the worst slums of London. He wore the rags of slum dwellers, begged lodging from them or slept in doorways and alleys. He worked with them when work was available and ate their meager fare. Then one day something happened, and it was suddenly discovered who he was. The king! The word spread like wildfire through the slums—this man who has been here and shared our life is the king! Many probably remembered things he had said and done, how uncomplaining he had been, how easy to know, how kind to children, how respectful to women. Everyone had loved him. Many could tell of ways in which he had helped them.

When his identity was discovered, the king returned to his palace. But things could never be the same again. Most of the lords and ladies of the palace were probably very upset. If the king did such a thing, they might be expected to do it! They would try hard to deny the story—to say it had never happened.

But what a change for the slum dwellers! The king whom they had feared, and sometimes hated because he was so remote, was now their friend. He knew them by name. He had eaten at their tables. A slum dweller could go to the palace and feel sure of a welcome. The king would call him by name, would listen to him, would help him. The people used to obey out of fear, now they would gladly die for such a king.

This is what the Bible tells us. God Almighty cared so much for us, his human children, that he left his heavenly palace and came to dwell among us. It is interesting to realize that in his own day, and to the present, it is chiefly the poor and the humble who first understood who Jesus was. The rulers of Jerusalem put him to death. The powerful of the earth often feel little need of him. But the oppressed, the lonely, the poor, the neglected seem always to recognize him first.

Lent and Holy Week are reminders of the king living in the slums of the world. The Resurrection—the Easter message—is the Bible's version of the discovery that this was, indeed, the king. The disciples and the early church knew the Resurrection as proof that Jesus was not just a good man, but was truly the Son of God.

As mortal, finite, often sinful human beings, can we use Lent as a time to think of how poor our lives would be if we knew only a God of power, whom we obeyed only through fear? Perhaps we can reread some of the Gospel stories of Jesus' love and concern for human beings. Then, perhaps we too can greet Easter with a renewed sense of joy and thanksgiving for the glorious good news that this Jesus whom we have come to know and love and trust is in reality the Almighty Creator of heaven and earth—God himself in human form—who knows us each by name, numbers the hairs of our heads, and welcomes us into an eternal fellowship in his kingdom.

Let us pray:

Open, we beseech you, our eyes to behold your goodness to us, your human children, revealed to us in the beauty of the world, in the love of family and friends, and above all in the life, death, and resurrection of Jesus Christ our Lord and Savior. May we learn to rejoice in the knowledge of your everlasting caring for us and for all humankind in this world and in the world to come. We ask this in Jesus' name. Amen.

Alice B. Mann

"Lazarus, Come Forth"

Jesus said, "I am the resurrection and I am life."

(John 11:25 NEB)

Then he raised his voice in a great cry: "Lazarus, come forth." The dead man came out, his hands and feet swathed in linen bands, his face wrapped in a cloth. Jesus said, "Loose him; let him go." (John 11:43–44 NEB)

The story from the Gospel of John of the raising of Lazarus is a very strange story. It is a story marked by resentment, hesitancy, irony, and the macabre. And yet, somehow, it is supposed to help us get ready for the passion and resurrection of our Lord. The raising of Lazarus is a strange story for the Fifth Sunday in Lent.

It is, first, a story of resentment. As Jesus arrives in Bethany, both Martha and Mary greet him with a bitter accusation: "Lord, if you had been here, my brother would not have died." Here is their Jesus, good friend of Lazarus, the one who has healed so many strangers and even brought to life a little girl he had never met. Here is the friend to whom they sent word that Lazarus was gravely ill, but who did not come until days later when it was too late.

And this Lazarus story is a story of hesitancy. When Jesus receives the message that Lazarus is sick, he replies that the illness will not end in death; and waits for two days before setting out for Bethany. Jesus seemed generally hesitant about miracles. We recall the story of the marriage feast at Cana, and Jesus' protest that his time had not yet come. And we remember from the First Sunday of Lent that Jesus refused to turn stones into bread. Jesus was not a very willing wonder-worker, and we can guess that he perceived very clearly how the people's demand for more and more miracles could distract him from the core of his ministry—his entry into Jerusalem, his passion, death, and resurrection.

Jesus seemed to use his power of healing only when he was confronted face to face by another human being begging him for help, and expressing great faith that Jesus had indeed the power to heal. Jesus, the very image of compassion, cannot refuse the one who stands in front of him. And Jesus, the living revelation of the loving power of God, cannot put the faith of the asker to any further test. So Jesus heals people. But here, just days before Passover time, the time of his passion and death, Jesus receives the message from Martha and Mary: his own dear friend is dying. If he goes, he will surely be called upon to heal once more, and there would once more be crowds and rumors and countless people bringing him their sick to heal. Jesus hesitates. Perhaps he is hoping that Lazarus may recover on his own. Or perhaps, as the Gospel writer suggests, he is aware that he will be called upon to raise Lazarus from the dead, and that this is part of the unfolding of his identity which is soon to come to its climax in the passion. But Jesus hesitates.

And the Lazarus story is an ironic one, in its own way. Lazarus is temporarily revived, but someday he will die, and Jesus will not be there, and the grieving will have to be done all over again. And in the sequel to the Lazarus story in the next chapter of the Gospel, we find that the high priests want to kill Lazarus, because he was causing many Jews to join the followers of Jesus.

Finally, the Lazarus story is a macabre one. This revival of a man four days dead, which on the surface ought to be the pinnacle of Jesus' healing ministry, is not only full of resentment, hesitancy, and irony, it is also more than a little morbid. When Jesus orders the stone rolled away, Martha makes one of her characteristically practical observations: "Lord, you can't do that because the tomb will smell."

This strange, complicated, distasteful resurrection story does in fact prepare us for Easter. But far from giving us a glimpse or foretaste of the glory of that feast, it prepares us with contrast and negative example. In it, we discover what a true resurrection faith is *not* about.

First of all, our resurrection faith as Christians is not *primarily* about miracles like the temporary revival of Lazarus. If it were, we would spend our whole life in a frenzy, asking the Lord to postpone just one more time the hardships and losses that belong to us as human beings. How far this is from the Jesus, who, when the hour had finally come to face Jerusalem, went resolutely toward the completion of his earthly ministry, toward the risk, the suffering, and even the death which it included. Resurrection faith has something to do with the *transformation* of our losses—ultimately our own death—not with the avoidance of them.

Second, resurrection faith is not *primarily* about the resurrection of the body on the last day. If it were, Martha's Jewish faith would seem adequate already, and there would seem to be no need for the life or death of Jesus at all. As Jews, Martha and Mary already believed in the resurrection on the last day. But for Mary and Martha, and for us too, the resurrection on the last day seems a distant abstract possibility in the face of present grief and hardship.

What then *is* a true resurrection faith about? Jesus says it all in one sentence. *I am the resurrection and I am life*. Jesus himself, speaking in the present tense, is here and now the reality of resurrection. Right here and right now in our lives, Jesus is calling us out of our tombs just as he called Lazarus, inviting us to participate in his victory over death.

What kinds of tombs do we live in? What kinds of death are we empowered to overcome right now? I believe that if each of us stops to think about it, we can begin to describe the walls of our own personal tombs in some detail, and in these next two weeks I would recommend this as the subject of at least a few minutes meditation. For those of you who are like me, and find any Lenten discipline of prayer and meditation very difficult to maintain, here, perhaps, is a manageable goal for the next two weeks—to spend *some time* meditating on the forms of death in which we live.

I cannot tell you what these will be. But I can suggest some possibilities.

One tomb might bear the shape of an emotional deadlock in a marriage, of our inclinations to demand that the other change first, or to refuse to seek outside help.

One tomb for a person alone might be resentment and self-pity.

One tomb might be a relentless drive to do things, to be busy, to achieve something, a drive which always gives us a good excuse for not responding humanly to the people around us.

One tomb for a young adult might be a desperate search for independence and intimacy which closes out both the support and the demands of any community.

One tomb for parents might be a sense of anxiety that adolescence may bring at the loss of relationships with their children, along with a loss of identity and meaning for the parents.

One tomb might be a pursuit of excellence that keeps myself and others exhausted with the fear that we might not meet the standards the next time.

One tomb might look like nostalgia, a persistent retreat into the past.

And one tomb might look like a nurturing of the doubtful, cynical sides of ourselves, and the avoidance of commitment which that allows. And that may be the darkest tomb of them all, because it is at that tomb that we would stop to question the very voice that would call us out.

As with Lazarus, Jesus is not only making a demand on us to come out of the tomb. He is at the same time empowering us to stand up and walk out, just as we are, still bound in our graveclothes. Lazarus is loosed from these *after* he emerges from the tomb; and so we cannot try to put off our resurrection—until we feel stronger, until the financial situation looks better, until the peak season is over, until we have finished therapy. Jesus calls us out now.

As was mentioned in our forum program on ancient liturgy several weeks ago, this Eucharist we celebrate today is a sharing with the Lord in a resurrection meal, just as the disciples shared food with Jesus several times between his resurrection and his ascension. The Lord who has left *his* tomb invites us to leave *our* tombs, right now, as we stand up from our pews to come to the altar rail.

He invites us, newly risen, to share with him, and in him, the bread of life.

LaVonne Althouse

Love's Winning Circle

Acts 10:34–43; Matthew 28:1–10

<small>EASTER</small>

The lessons for Easter Day, that happiest as well as holiest day for Christians, call to mind a poem by Edwin Markham because these lessons, together, do what the poem describes:

> He drew a circle that shut me out—
> Heretic, rebel, a thing to flout.
> But Love and I had the wit to win:
> We drew a circle that took him in!

If *love* is the verb that names God for us because in that verb we encounter God's most characteristic action, then Markham's poem describes God's action in Christ on that first Easter Day. During the past week we have seen how the world drew a circle that shut Jesus out as a heretic and rebel—one who threatened the religious establishment of his day and one who was convicted of threatening Roman authority. (Only when convicted of that sort of high treason could Jesus have been crucified.)

But love, which is God's action in the world and in Christ, had the wit to win. Our lessons illustrate two actions, two events of history, in which this love drew a circle large enough finally to include the whole world in the salvation Christ offers.

The most remarkable feature of the Gospel, which focuses

65

on Easter morning events, is that God's Holy Spirit moved two *women* to go to the tomb at dawn, and the risen Christ appeared first to two *women* whom he then sent to tell his disciples that he was alive, and where he would next meet them. (All four Gospels are remarkable in that one or two or three or several women, depending on which Gospel you are reading, are first to discover the empty tomb. Mary Magdalene is always the first witness; she alone, in both Mark's and John's Gospel, is first to meet the risen Lord.)

Both Mark and Luke record that the disciples refused to believe the women. We know that in Jewish society no one ever accepted testimony of women as officially valid or true; it had no status in court. So it is curious that Matthew, who was always concerned to show how Jesus fulfilled the law and the prophets, is the only Gospel writer who tells of *two women* finding the empty tomb and of *two women* being the first to see the Lord alive again. (You may remember in Jewish courts the testimony of *two men*, who were eyewitnesses and who agreed completely, was needed to confirm any point or convict anyone charged with wrongdoing.) For some reason which no one has explained, Matthew either ignores or sets aside or deliberately confronts the stipulation that the two confirming witnesses must be men; he shows us two women finding the tomb, learning of the resurrection, meeting Jesus, and bearing his message and his instructions to the disciples to meet him in Galilee.

Positively delightful is Matthew's account of the events at the tomb as the women arrive. After a great earthquake an angel appears. The event so terrifies the tomb guards that they faint dead away, this in spite of the fact that they are seasoned veterans of that army which conquered all the known world at that time and maintained Rome's authority in the conquered lands—the U.S. Marines or British Navy of the first century. Moreover, the penalty for dereliction of duty, the charge they would face, was death. The two women, by contrast, though possibly shaken, retained enough self-possession to hear the angel's message, turn around, and hurry to tell the disciples the news. Even meeting the risen Christ only impelled them more eagerly to seek the disciples and to share the story with them. (That may not blow your mind, but it surely should blow all myths about a "weaker sex" out the nearest window.)

Most surprising, the disciples do not for a moment doubt the women, but begin immediately packing for the day-or-so journey north to Galilee to meet the Lord. And so Christ closes the circle of events which began when he was hailed as king of Palm Sunday—and climaxed when he took twelve men to share his last meal on earth on Thursday—by appearing first as risen Lord to women, and by sending two women to testify that he lives. The circle, thus enlarged as a faith event, confirms Paul's testimony that in Christ there is neither male nor female, but we are all one. The circle of witnesses now includes Jewish women as well as Jewish men.

But where does that leave us who, with our ancestors, are gentiles? We must look to the lesson from Acts where Luke testifies to numerous events that show the circle drawn larger, including more of the world that on Good Friday rejected Jesus. The visit to Cornelius marks the first time Peter—to whom all authority in heaven and earth was given by Jesus on the mountain where the transfiguration happened (according to Matthew)—baptized an uncircumcised gentile. What Peter says to Cornelius in Acts 10:34 is, to us who are gentiles, the most precious verse of all in the New Testament. For Cornelius is the first person like ourselves to be baptized by a disciple and received as a member of the body of Christ. In the Middle East, Christians refer to this story as the Gentile Pentecost. (Remember that on Pentecost the gospel was preached only to Jews from all parts of the world who were in Jerusalem. With Cornelius the *goyim*— those who belong to the other nations—may also become members of Christ's body.)

You probably remember that Peter was sent to Cornelius after he had a vision of "unclean" food which a voice bade him eat, and charged him: "What I have made clean, you shall not call unclean." In baptizing Cornelius, Peter enables Christ to draw the circle large enough to include the whole world that had rejected Jesus of Nazareth. This is the faith event, the second of our two actions, that confirms Paul's testimony that in Christ there is neither Jew nor Greek but we are all one.

When the risen Christ meets the two women, the first human beings to whom he speaks after rising, he greets them with a Greek word meaning "rejoice!" And this resurrection gives us at least three blessings at which we rejoice.

First, the resurrection overcomes not only death, but all the arrogance of authority used cruelly to repress the timidity of frightened followers who fear to witness to Christ's power. And it overcomes the unthinking injustice into which masses of people can be manipulated—masses who are indifferent to suffering and unaware and unconcerned about the consequences of their actions. This victory over all arrogant authority, unfaithful timidity, and unthinking injustice is Christ's first blessing as risen Lord.

The second blessing is the gift of the Holy Spirit sent to empower us to take courage and proclaim Christ, the victory of his resurrection, and the justice, concern and love of God for all people which that resurrection triumphantly shows.

The third blessing at which we rejoice is that Christ has made it possible for people in all the world to become members of the family that knows him, the power of his resurrection, the security of his love, and the universality of his justice. Through the women we are called to rejoice; by the commandment to go into all the world, each of us is personally charged to share in telling all people everywhere what happened on that first Easter morning. We too are impelled to declare how the event of that morning comforts and strengthens each of us, melts all our fears, loneliness, and sorrow, and heals all our grief and pain. For Christ has drawn a large circle that includes all the world. And we cannot wait to tell others the joyful news we have received.

Phyllis Trible

The Opportunity of Loneliness

Jeremiah 1:4–10

THE ORDINATION OF MARY BEALE

The prophet Jeremiah is our guide and interpreter for this
unique event in the life of Mary Beale, and in the life of this
church. Hear now the words of the prophet as they travel
across the centuries to confront us in this time and place:

> Now the word of the Lord came to me saying,
> "Before I formed you in the womb I knew you,
> and before you were born I set you apart;
> I appointed you a prophet to the nations."
> Then I said, "Ah, Lord God! Behold, I do not know how to
>   speak, for I am only a youth." But the Lord said to me,
> "Do not say, 'I am only a youth';
> for to all to whom I send you you shall go,
> and whatever I command you you shall speak.
> Be not afraid of them,
> for I am with you to deliver you,
>   says the Lord."
> Then the Lord put forth his hand and touched my mouth; and
>   the Lord said to me,
> "Behold, I have put my words in your mouth.
> See, I have set you this day over nations and over kingdoms,
>   to pluck up and break down,
>   to destroy and to overthrow,
>   to build and to plant."   (Jer. 1:4–10)

Jeremiah speaks to us out of the mystery of origin and
destiny—mystery which makes its claim upon him while not
deigning to give explanations, answers, controls, or reasons:

70

"Before I formed you in the womb I knew you,
and before you were born I set you apart."

Set-apartness. Therein lies the root of the thing which was to plague Jeremiah all his life, as he stood on the boundary between two worlds: a world of crumbling assurances and a world of impending exile. The tiny kingdom of Judah, with its noble heritage, secure in the promises of a Davidic dynasty which would last forever, and blessed as a nation under God—this kingdom moved inexorably to defeat and captivity. And it is Jeremiah who is set apart to name the demise, to declare it the will of a God who was not supposed to act that way, and thereby to bring upon himself the wrath of his friends and to know the silence and hostility of God.

This set-apartness, which he cannot escape, is experienced as dreadful loneliness:

> I did not sit in the company of merrymakers,
>   nor did I rejoice;
> I sat alone, because thy hand was upon me,
>   for thou hadst filled me with indignation.
> Why is my pain unceasing,
>   my wound incurable,
>   refusing to be healed?
> Wilt thou be to me like a deceitful brook,
>   like waters that fail?   (15:17–18)

This is a terrible loneliness which touches all of us in the depths of existence. It is the loneliness of our father Abraham and our mother Sarah, uprooted from family and from land, going forth without models or road maps, because the command has come. It is the loneliness of a Moabite woman, Ruth, breaking with her personal and corporate history, to dwell among a foreign people and to choose a foreign god. It is the loneliness of Jesus, set apart on a cross, high and lifted up, crying out, "My God, my God, why hast thou forsaken me?"

Mary Beale is set apart for the ministry in an age when the church stands on the boundary, when it has failed to be true to its meaning under God, when it moves inexorably into exile. And she too will know the loneliness of being set apart: "Why, Mary, you don't look old enough to be a minister," some will say. And Mary will know the loneliness of age. "Why, Mary, you're too pretty to be a clergy*man*!" So runs that ugly compliment which isolates, alienates, and objectifies a human being; the loneliness of beauty intertwined with the loneliness of sex. Mary is set apart to witness to truth and to freedom in a male bastion called the church, a bastion none too eager to free itself of the sin of sexism. And there is for her also the set-apartness of time and place—the loneliness of new beginnings—of leaving the freedom of student life, the delights of the city, the joys of friends in familiar surroundings.

Set apart by a God who may come in silence or even in enmity.

There is a terrible loneliness in ordination, but ordination has no monopoly on loneliness. Each of us bearing a name is set apart. We know loneliness and we know the *temptation* of loneliness, for loneliness breeds self-centeredness even as self-centeredness produces loneliness.

> And before you were born I set you apart; I appointed you a prophet to the nations.

> Then I said, "Ah, Lord God! Behold, I do not know how to speak, for I am only a youth."

Why, O God, do you set us apart? Why, O God, do you pick on me? I have no distinctive qualifications for ordination. I am only a youth. I am only a man. No, I am only a woman. I am an average student and do not deserve set-apartness. I am a superior student and do not deserve loneliness. I, I, I—the seduction of self occasioned by that set-apartness which marks all human existence.

This disease of ego runs like a thread throughout the biblical narratives. Moses was infected, boasting before God even as he complained, "Who am I that I should go to Pharaoh and bring the children of Israel out of Egypt?" Elijah, set apart against the prophets of Baal on Mt. Carmel, bragging as he lamented, "I am the only faithful one left." Jonah, so full of anger that his nostrils burned, turned his call as a witness to mercy and grace into an occasion of seeking self-confirmation in death. "Anger is good for me even unto death." Paul too was no stranger to the temptation of set-apartness, and Jeremiah suffered from it perhaps most of all:

> O Lord, thou knowest;
>> remember me and visit me,
>> and take vengeance for me on my persecutors.
> In thy forbearance take me not away;
>> know that for thy sake I bear reproach. (15:15)

Loneliness breeds self-centeredness. The more we insist upon it—and we can insist upon it by fighting against it as well as by giving in to it—the more we drag ourselves deeper and deeper into the abyss of ego. So many of our current clichés about life and its meaning are but subtle and sophisticated variations of this disease. Identity crisis, for example, is a misguided concern with self. Encounter groups, encouraging us to express ourselves, to affirm ourselves, are similar symptoms of a deep disease. Christians of another age did not hesitate to label these concerns as the deadly sin of pride. We whitewash that sin now by calling it self-respect or, turning the coin, we talk about feelings of inferiority and insecurity—all inverse witnesses to self. Thus the demon of ego persists as the monster we manufacture in response to set-apartness:

Ah, Lord God! Behold, *I* do not know how to speak,
for *I* am only a youth.''

The reply of *faith* to the egocentrism of loneliness is
clear, unambiguous, and uncompromising:

Do not say, ''I am only a youth'';
For to all to whom I send you you shall go,
and whatever I command you you shall speak.

Erase your ego, Jeremiah. Or in the words of Norman O.
Brown, ''The answer to the identity crisis is: get lost.'' Or in
the words of Jesus, ''If anyone would come after me, let that
one die to self; let that one lift up the cross: let that one
crucify the ego.'' We live not to express ourselves; we are set
apart not to wallow in self-pity or in self-respect, but rather
to go where we are sent, to speak what we are commanded,
to do the will not of self and not of others but of the One who
creates us and breathes into us from moment to moment.

For faith, then, loneliness, set-apartness, is the opportunity to discover the roots of our being in transcendent love. It
is Abraham and Sarah, set apart from the past, receiving the
gift of land. It is Ruth, stranger in a foreign land, discovering
the providence of the God who blesses. It is Elijah, hearing
beyond his selfish lament the voice of gentle silence—the
silence which creates, loves, and sends us forth. The opportunity of loneliness is the movement from the cry of dereliction, ''My God, My God, why hast thou forsaken me?'' to
the awareness of divine presence: ''Lo, I am with you always.'' A crucified ego is resurrected love.

Set apart in birth, set apart in destiny, we know who we are
by letting go of our claims to identity:

''Do not say, I am . . .''

Bear witness not to self. As for others, bear witness not to
them either:

"Be not afraid of them, Jeremiah."

That threatening "them"—the selves of others—as ready to ensnare us as the temptations of our own ego:

"Be not afraid of them, Mary."

For the assurance and witness of faith is deliverance by divine presence, not by self and not by others:

"Be not afraid of them for *I am* with you to deliver you."

This *I AM* stands over against the I am of self and others. This *I AM* is that understanding and love which gives us birth, which sustains us, which heals us, which frees us to be loving and understanding human beings, not enslaved by one another.

In origin and in destiny, Jeremiah knew loneliness. In that knowledge, he moved from the pit of egocentrism to deliverance by transcendent presence. And thus he instructs us on this day when Mary is set apart for love, for truth, and for understanding; on this day when all of us acknowledge our shared loneliness in order to move beyond ourselves to embrace and participate in love. Loneliness understood is liberating love. For this, we are all set apart this day.

O God of Abraham, Isaac, and Jacob,
O God of Sarah, Rebekah, and Rachel,
May thy will be done in the life of Mary as in the lives of us all set apart by thee.

In the name of Jesus, the Christ. Amen.

Carter Heyward

Priesthood

Matthew 9:36–38

THE ORDINATION OF DOUG CLARK

Introduction

In the spring of 1974, the people (laity and clergy) of St. Mary's Episcopal Church in the Manhattanville section of Harlem asked that its three deacons—all seminary graduates and candidates for the priesthood, duly examined and found fully qualified for ordination—be ordained to the priesthood together in the parish, on May 17. After much correspondence and conversation, two of the three of us were turned down, with regrets, by the Bishop and Standing Committee of the Diocese of New York because we were female. At that point, the male deacon asked me to preach *his* ordination to the priesthood, in St. Mary's, on May 17.

Less than three months later, eleven women deacons were ordained to the priesthood by three bishops. A year later, four more women deacons were ordained priests. All fifteen of us were deemed "invalid" by the bishops of the church, and the bishops who had ordained us were censured for their action. None of the fifteen of us, nor our congregations and others with whom we worked, accepted the ruling of "invalidity," but rather we worked as priests of the church in whatever ways we were able to, often underground.

76

In September 1976, the Episcopal Church opened the ordained priesthood to women.

As I reread my sermon on Priesthood—written and preached before my own ordination as a priest, of course—I can affirm it today with even greater gusto.

When he saw the crowds, he had compassion for them, because they were harassed and helpless, like sheep without a shepherd. Then he said to his disciples, "The harvest is plentiful, but the laborers are few; pray therefore the Lord of the harvest to send out laborers into his harvest."

(Matt. 9:36–38)

In the name of God—Creator, Redeemer, Sustainer. Amen.

Priesthood

Tonight we celebrate the ordination of one of us, Doug Clark, to the priesthood. Affirming the priesthood of all believers, as I do, I believe that all of us as priests have come together to designate one of our brothers as a priest, in no way different from us, except inasmuch as tonight Doug is making a commitment to the priesthood as his vocation. All of us are priests, by baptism. Tonight Doug will become a priest, by ordination, henceforth marked by his commitment to priesthood as central to his vocation, his profession, his life.

What is a priest?

When our Lord looked out and saw the people, he felt sorry for them, for us, because we were harassed and dejected, confused and afraid, like sheep without a shepherd. Like people without a God. Then God said to the disciples: "The harvest is rich, but the laborers are few. Too few people have committed themselves to tending the harvest. So ask the Lord of the harvest to send laborers to his harvest."

Pray to God that men *and* women will be sent.

Pray to God that women and men will be priests, joining hands as a priesthood of believers in God—lay people and clergy committed to helping brothers and sisters recognize the God who moves through and among them, as a shepherd moves among sheep, caring and prodding.

A priest is one of the sheep, one of the sheep who is aware of the presence of the shepherd and who continually nudges other sheep into obedience to the shepherd—God.

A priest is a person given authority by God to help other people realize that God is their authority.

A priest is one called by God to spend his or her life helping others believe that they too are called by God to spend their lives helping others see that they too are called by God . . .

A priest is one who sees, or hears, or is otherwise aware of the Spirit of God moving within and among human beings and who is committed to helping all human beings become aware of God's Spirit within and among them.

Hence, a priest knows that to take God seriously entails taking oneself and other human beings seriously. A priest is committed to human growth and self-esteem for all people; to healing and comforting; to preaching and teaching; to prophecy and action, in order that people may have self-esteem and may see that others have it—all in the name of God, who, incarnate, shows us in no subtle way through the life of Jesus that if God is taken seriously, human beings will be taken seriously. "For inasmuch as you did it to one of my brothers, or sisters, you did it to me."

All of us are called to this priesthood—black and white, young and old, male and female.

Ordination

An ordained priest in the Episcopal Church is a man, recognized, educated, and accepted by the church as a person who can help us recognize our own priesthoods.

An ordained priest is a man who has accepted God's call and the church's designation of him as its priest by the laying on of hands by a bishop, who symbolizes the continuity of the Catholic church's traditional priesthood. Thus, the ordained priest is said to be part of the "apostolic succession," an unbroken succession of men who have been ordained as priests, a succession rooted in Jesus' charge to Peter that he be "the rock" on which the church be built. Continuity is meaningful; irresponsible allegiance to tradition is not. Both Doug and I have trouble with the sort of ecclesiastical irresponsibility that would lead us, or you, into believing that an ordained priest has actually been somehow "zapped" by God and set apart from the rest of the Christian community, usually on a pedestal.

We have trouble with such a notion because it is arrogant and idolatrous. It rings of insecurity and ego-tripping on the part of priests who see themselves in this way. And it rings of hero-worshiping and irresponsible dependency on the part of lay people who view priests in this way. Most significantly, this pedestal view of priesthood deprives *all* Christians of having to assume responsibility for our own lives, our own faith, and our own participation in the priesthood of the church.

An ordained priest is not set apart. He is in the midst of the people, although preferably not often in the center; he moves with them back and forth, in and out, between the center and the boundaries of church life, activity, and decision making.

Nor is the ordained priest set above the rest of the people. He is right beside them.

The ordained priest is a sacramental person, one who knows that every Eucharist is, for example, an outward and visible sign of God's grace that re-creates and binds humankind as one body. The bread and the wine are signs of the body and blood of Jesus Christ who is alive, suffering, dying, rising, and present within and among all human beings. The ordained priest knows this, so he celebrates it—as do all Christians!

The ordained priest is the official "celebrant" of the Eucharist, I believe, not because the priest alone *can* celebrate it, nor because it is God's will that the priest, and the priest alone, perform some sort of "magic act" at the altar. The ordained priest is the celebrant because the church expects it of him—quite simply that. Such expectation is rooted in ecclesiastical polity, not in divine law writ large.

There is no magic act at the altar. There is divine activity and there is human activity, which are coexistent in mystical relationship everywhere all the time. This is sacrament, not magic—be it at the altar or on the streets of West Harlem.

Which is all to say, Doug, that I do not believe you are being "zapped" tonight. I do not believe your ontology, your essential mode of being, will be changed as you are ordained priest. You will not be set apart or above. You will not be endowed with magical powers. You will be no more special, no more Christ-like, no less a deacon, no less human, no other Doug than you are right now. You will, in fact, be no more priest than you are right now, or than the others of us in this congregation.

The difference will lie in the church's *acceptance* and *confirmation* of your call to priesthood as vocation. You have, I suspect, known your own priesthood for months or years. Tonight the Episcopal Church will recognize it. And this is what we celebrate.

Conformity

Doug, you have just taken and signed an oath in which you stated that you believe the Old and New Testaments to be the word of God and to contain all things therein necessary to salvation and you furthermore engaged yourself to "conform to the doctrine, discipline, and worship" of the Episcopal Church. This oath is worth addressing.

It is clear to me that such "conformity," rooted in obedience to the God of history elucidated in the Bible, can be
rightly expected of all Episcopal clergy. When grounded in
the gospel, our conformity is our strength and is central to
the workings of a creative church. But it is also clear to me
that conformity to anything less than the gospel cannot be
rightly expected of Episcopal clergy, or any other Christians. Furthermore, that such ungodly conformity is
anathema to all that is just, decent, holy.

Thus, Doug, you will find, I am sure, that there will be
times when conformity to stated doctrine, discipline, or worship will be unthinkable for you, just as many people have
discovered that conformity to unjust or destructive secular
laws has been impossible for them, precisely because of their
conformity to the Christian gospel.

And so the burden of Christian conscience, emerging from
your understanding of what God is about in the world and
church, will fall upon your shoulders many times as you
attempt to decide what to do; whom to obey; how seriously
to take a certain church law or teaching; how seriously to
take a secular law in light of church teachings; what the cost
may be for you; how much you will risk; and on what basis
you are making your decisions.

It is at this point that the first part of the "oath of
conformity"—in which you essentially pledge yourself to
biblical teachings, presumably as they relate to life in today's
world—must if necessary take precedence over the doctrine,
discipline, and worship of the Episcopal Church. *And* it is at
this point that the life and death and resurrection of Jesus
become the authority for your conformity:

Jesus—the Great High Priest, who never claimed to be a
high priest.

Jesus—who constantly pointed away from himself towards God; and who might well look with dismay upon the

church's tendency to authoritatively idolize itself as his body, rather than to point away from itself towards a living, moving, active God, an authority who cannot be contained fully in any doctrine or tradition or religion, including Christianity.

Jesus—a human being who cared enough about his brothers and sisters to put them, consistently, above the doctrine, discipline, and worship of his own religious community.

Jesus—who responded to human need, praying, healing, feeding, comforting, rebuking, teaching, living, and dying without much regard for how the world would or would not respond to him.

Jesus—for whom rejection, suffering, and death were inevitable.

Jesus Christ—the Great High Priest—to whom, in the last analysis, our conformity is accountable.

Yes, Doug, I imagine you will be disliked by some, perhaps by many, if you conform to your understanding of the holy gospel which is God's business.

Vocation

I think it is significant that you have chosen to combine your priesthood with psychotherapy. Important, because your own vocation will embrace the interrelationship between spiritual perspective and the emotional stuff out of which human experience is in large part shaped, felt, and coped with. My point here is *not* that there actually exist two levels of reality—one sacred and one profane; rather, that there exists, sacramentally, *one* reality—seen and named in different ways by different people for different reasons. *Spiritual, emotional, mental, intellectual, social,* and *political* can be, for example, words descriptive of a single reality. Hence, God is not set apart from psychotherapy. God is *in* the psychotherapeutic process—God working through you, the therapist, and through the other person, towards healing. A holy process.

There is no political problem—be it war, Watergate, racism, sexism, crime, or poverty—that is not also a critical religious problem to be taken seriously by the church. By the priest and the therapist.

Likewise, there is no such thing as a purely "theological" problem or "ecclesiastical" problem that does not relate, profoundly, to some social, political, psychological, or otherwise inadequately categorized dilemma in the larger world. The priest's task is not to "combine" religion, politics, and therapy. They *are combined*, by the grace of God. Our task, as priests, is to acknowledge this, and marvel at it. To question it, and probe it. And to preach, teach, counsel, administer, and live on this assumption, knowing well that *every service of worship is a political demonstration;* and that *every political demonstration is a liturgy*. And that, whatever the occasion, therapy is in process.

So, the church cannot beg theological immunity from facing head-on either the rest of the world's problems, or its own problems as it reflects, and helps perpetuate, crises of injustice, prejudice, and despair in the world. Not only can we not, as Christians, beg theological immunity, but we as Christians are called to prophetic leadership towards solutions of such problems, be they beyond or within the walls of the church.

St. Mary's is perhaps an ideal place for both you and me to be learning what it means to be priest, pastor, prophet. Because the people here—clergy and laity—expect no less from us, or from themselves.

Doug, the past few months—the coincidence of our meeting, your coming to St. Mary's, our times together in the liturgy, at lunch, laughing, more recently sharing mutual pain—have led me to consider what a remarkable time this has been for us. I like you. You are a loving, talented, committed, and very human person.

And as you know, my sister deacons and I are not being ordained tonight because we are female. I cannot and should not hide my anger about our situation, any more than I would if I were told that someone here tonight could not be ordained a priest because he or she was black—and because the national church "happened to have" this ruling about black people.

Tonight (17 May 1974) marks to the day the twentieth anniversary of the now-celebrated Topeka vs. Brown decision of the Supreme Court, in which it ruled that "separate-but-equal" education is "inherently unequal." Twenty years comprise only a bare beginning towards black equality in America. A separate-but-equal mind-set still pervades in this country.

Similarly, a "separate-but-equal" theology has long undergirded the exclusion of women from full participation in the life and ministry of the church. That we Episcopalians—as a diocese, as a parish, as individuals—can comply for one more day with this blatant and fear-tinted discrimination, upheld by our national church legislators *against all women*, is outrageous to basic Christian and human sensibilities.

But there is something else I cannot and should not fail to say: I am aware here tonight of a Holy Spirit weaving its way among us all, binding us together in strange ways if only momentarily. Not negating the excitement or the anger, the pain or the ambivalence, but rather weaving these very human feelings into a larger, complexly patterned fabric of *faith* and *history*.

In faith and at this very moment in history, this group of people in St. Mary's is vibrating—in our differences; in our

consciences; uncomfortably, impatiently, confusedly, rest-
lessly, courageously; in gratitude for Doug's ministry, and in
awareness that the service itself is embodying perfect irony.

There is joy here. There is pain. There is energy here.
There is exhaustion. There is anticipation here. There is
dread. There is death. There is life here.

I close here, offering you, Doug, words that spring out of
my reflections on our vocation:

Doug, know that there is a God.
Face and embrace, do not flee from, your doubts.
Pray.
Accept and be yourself. Help others to do the same.
Forget about perfection and marvel at humanness.
Forget about others' definitions of what makes a "good man"
    or a "good priest."
Have courage and do what you must.
Do it wholeheartedly.
Rest and play. Laugh and cry.
Change and grow. Live and die.
Leave room for surprises!
Go in peace.
And if you don't try too hard to understand that peace, you
    will be free.
You're a beautiful person, Doug.
You are a priest.

By the grace, and in the name of God. Amen.

Letty Russell

The Impossible Possibility

Isaiah 52:13–15; Mark 10:35–45

In my undergraduate days at Wellesley College, I used to process with the choir at daily and Sunday chapel, up the aisle, toward a chancel where the words *non ministrari, sed ministrare* were written in huge letters across the upper wall. Each time I looked at those words, no matter how bleary-eyed or distractedly, I believed—believed that this lifestyle of Jesus, not to be ministered unto, but to minister, had something to do with my own lifestyle and with the reason why I was at college.

Today the words, although in modern English, are still with us. Our text, Mark 10:45 reads, ". . . not to be served, but to serve." But for all of us, I think, they have become more of a problem than a possibility:

> They are a problem for Christians because the very word *service* has become so debased in our culture that most people think of it, at best, as a sort of Band-Aid approach to helping others and, at worse, a cop-out from working for a just society.
>
> They are a problem for women, blacks, and other Third World groups because *service* is identified with subordination, powerlessness, and oppression.
>
> They are a problem for ministers and laity because we have created a class of professional "ministers" who

serve in structures which deprive the whole people of God of their own responsible servanthood or ministry. Yet here are the words:

And Jesus called them to him and said to them, "You know that those who are supposed to rule over the Gentiles lord it over them, and their great men exercise authority over them. But it shall not be so among you; but whoever would be great among you must be your servant, and whoever would be first among you must be slave of all. For the Son of man also came not to be served but to serve, and to give his life as a ransom for many." (Mark 10:42–45)

And here is the lifestyle of Jesus of Nazareth who came to serve and give his life as a ransom for the world. This impos-sible idea of service is in fact the only possibility for those who would follow Jesus.

This seemingly impossible role of service is possible for us all because it is not just a command. It is a gift of God.

Service is God's gift because it is God who serves us. Think of it. This God of the Hebrew-Christian tradition is like no other gods! God is the one who chooses to serve, not just to be worshiped or adored. Other gods have been re-vealed so that women and men could serve them. This God, the God of the Suffering Servant—the God of Jesus Christ, begins from the other end. God comes to the people, to liberate them so that they may celebrate their freedom by sharing it with others. In God's service, we see what Karl Barth calls the humanity of God. God is, first of all, not a king sitting on a pyramid of the world creating pyramids of domi-nation and subjugation in the hierarchies of church and soci-ety. Rather, the humanity of God is seen in that God chooses to be related to human beings through service.

No wonder our lesson from Isaiah says that the servant of Yahweh will startle the nations:

> —his appearance was so marred, beyond human
>   semblance,
> and his form beyond that of the sons of men—
> so shall he startle many nations;
>   kings shall shut their mouths because of him.
>
> (Isa. 52:14–15)

The servant cannot even be recognized because suffering service is not expected of a messianic figure by those in high places!

Service is also God's gift because Jesus not only calls his disciples to serve, he also provides the power and possibility of carrying this out.

In Jesus Christ we have the representation of a new humanity—the beginning of a new type of human being whose life is lived for others. Jesus came as Immanuel, God with us: to be with all people—the women as well as the men; the ignorant as well as the learned; the outcasts as well as the religiously acceptable; the oppressed as well as the oppressors. Jesus helps us to see the humanity of God so that we too can become representatives of new humanity. Here we see what it means to be truly and newly human. This is the image of God—freedom to serve others. This is the image into which humanity is created and redeemed. The whole story of the New Testament revolves around this one theme—diakonia, service. At last someone has come, not to be served but to serve! "Everything that was done by this Son of Man . . . including humiliation, self-emptying, cross, death, is summarized in one final communiqué": service.* This communiqué is offered as gift and promise. The disciples of Jesus are called to be servants, to be liberated for others.

---

*Hans Hoekendijk, *Horizons of Hope*, (Nashville: Tidings, 1970), p. 30.

God's intention for us now is just such an impossible possibility. Through service, God's and ours, we are liberated to be full human beings.

First, we are liberated for ministry, diakonia. We are set free from hierarchical structures which place ministry in the hands of a few to begin carrying out the work of the people.

Traditionally, diakonia has taken three forms: curative, preventive, and prospective.

—Curative diakonia is the healing and helping of victims in society.

—Preventive diakonia is the attempt to curtail the development of social ills which victimize human life.

—Prospective diakonia is the attempt to open the situation for a free realization and actualization of human life.

Although in the past the church has specialized in individual curative or Band-Aid tasks, people recently have become aware that it is necessary to work together on preventive health and social programs. The church has also become slowly involved in prospective programs in which society is so changed that people can take part in shaping their own destiny and that evils such as war, poverty, racism, and sexism can be attacked.

The kind of diakonia that we want in our own life is the latter. We do not want to be helped after we are crushed; we would rather have justice that leads to elimination of destructive social structures.

In being liberated for ministry, we are drawn first into the struggle for liberation of all peoples. Men and women, black and white, rich and poor seek to move together toward new ways of life in which those who have been oppressed are free to form their own agenda, to participate in shaping their own future, and to decide whom and how they will serve.

Second, we are liberated for others because we are called to be God's helpers or co-servants. This is the image of woman in Genesis 2. She is created by God as *'ezer,* a divine helper for man who needs to live and work in community. Just like the image of the *'ebed Yahweh,* the Servant of God, in Isaiah 52, woman—and also man—is seen as a human being who has been given the privilege of living for others as God's representative. This service in no way implies subordination. Nor does it imply domination of any human being over another. The alternative to subordination is not domination but service. There is no true ministry which is not freely given, in the same way that God's ministry is freely given. Social and church structures in which domination is used to make others serve are a denial of freedom, just as subordination is a denial of true human dignity.

In this respect, the work of the women's liberation movement and Third World liberation movements for new structures of justice, partnership, and sharing sometimes may be disruptive in family, church, and society. But they are not the real troublemakers. In fact, they are causing us to become aware of the real troublemakers—the structures of domination and subordination which destroy the possibility of true humanity and service.

Third, we are liberated for God because we can experience the love and service of God in our own lives. When confronted by the authorities, Peter boldly proclaimed, "We must obey God rather than men" (Acts 5:29). For the gospel claims our allegiance to the One who serves, beyond any human ideology; beyond any church or social structure.

Such a demand is not easy. It often makes us unreliable in a cause; unable to assert that, in fact, any particular program or organization is of ultimate significance. Because Christians seek to live according to a new way of being human, they often find themselves as marginal or misfit people in the games of dominance and exploitation that people play. If we are not misfits, then we need to have another look at how and where we serve.

In the last few years many women have been discovering that they really are misfits and marginal to the male-dominated society in which they live. Some are seeking new ways to go on being misfits for the sake of society. They are working in community with others on the boundaries of institutions where they can try to create new structures for human life. My own experience is that I have always been a misfit, and I am glad to find other women and men who feel as I do—those who are seeking, not just to be part of things as they are, but to serve the process of change toward God's intended future.

Not to be served, but to serve. These words—so impossibly possible as a gift of God—are an instant communiqué concerning who we are, and where we are going as followers of Christ and as representatives of an emerging new humanity in which "There is neither Jew nor Greek, there is neither slave nor free, there is neither male nor female" (Gal. 3:28).

Long ago, as I glibly read those words circling that chapel chancel—*non ministrari, sed ministrare*—I didn't know how tough service would be! I didn't know just how much that promise of Jesus meant. I tried to share his baptism and temptations and I often ended up with wrong answers and worse defeats.

I still don't know how much that promise means. But I do know that in spite of all the devaluation and misuse and betrayal of the word *service* in churches and society, these words of Jesus continue to lead us toward a life of freedom. They are words about *a revolution in which everyone wins*—in which everyone finds a way of ministry and partnership on the road to human freedom!

Rosemary Radford Ruether

You Shall Call No Man Father: Sexism, Hierarchy and Liberation

Matthew 23:1–12

My attention was called to this text of Matthew by a somewhat amusing incident which took place several years ago during the ordination of eleven women to the priesthood of the Episcopal Church in Philadelphia. There is a place in the liturgy of ordination for those present to express their objections to the proceedings. The crowd that gathered there was very enthusiastic, so there was not much objection, but a few people had come there to protest. One young priest took the mike and said in a sonorous voice: "Jesus broke many rules, but one rule he did not break. You shall call God, Father, and his priests shall be called Father too." There was a gasp of surprise and muffled laughter in the congregation since many remembered the text somewhat more accurately and knew that it said something rather different! This incident drew my attention to this and other texts in the Synoptics where Jesus puts down hierarchical concepts of leadership in the Christian movement.

The first thing we Christians need to get past in studying this text is the tendency to think that Jesus was just criticizing some bad attitudes characteristic of "Jews" and "Judaism." Jesus was criticizing his own religious community, not standing outside of Judaism. He was criticizing tendencies to use leadership for power and prestige. So if we are to translate the meaning of these sayings correctly to our own situation, we have to apply them in a similar way to our own Christian communities. We should read the text as saying something like this:

> The clergy and the theologians take their stand on the Bible, but they don't practice what they preach. Instead they like to wear elegant cassocks and fringed vestments, and to be called Reverend and Your Excellency.
>
> But don't let people call you Doctor or Reverend or Father, because your relationship to God should do away with all such titles and power relations among you and make you sisters and brothers toward one another. Those who are leaders show their leadership by service, not by power and dominance.

Once we read this text as a criticism of our own community, then we begin to realize that Jesus is proposing nothing less than a revolution in the very nature of leadership and its relationship to community. The relationship of God to creation or of Christ to the church does not establish a hierarchy which is to be imitated as the pattern of dominance and submission in the church. Rather God and Christ overthrow such power relations, because Christ himself sets a new pattern as one who empties himself and becomes a servant (Phil. 2:7). Relations between Christians are thereby established as communal, relations of brothers and sisters, not relations of fathers and children, or masters and servants. Those who would imitate Jesus must imitate this servanthood, and not seize upon leadership as mastery. When the sons of Zebedee foolishly imagine that the establishment of Jesus' kingdom means that they will share in positions of power and rule others "on his right side and on his left," like worldly rulers, Jesus rebukes them, saying:

> You know that the rulers of the Gentiles lord it over them,
> and their great men exercise authority over them. It shall not
> be so among you; but whoever would be great among you
> must be your servant, and whoever would be first among you
> must be your slave, even as the Son of man came not to be
> served, but to serve, and to give his life as ransom for many.
>
> (Matt. 20:25–28)

Texts that establish the Christian leadership as one of service have tended to become mystified in the course of history. On the one hand, the church has used the title "minister" and "servant" for its leadership, while in fact developing princely and hierarchical power roles for these servants. The revolutionary meaning in the word *minister* is lost precisely as it becomes a title of power! The bishop who calls himself "Servant of the People of God" and brings up the rear of the procession is not being humble, but using gestures of humility as the ultimate sanctification of ecclesiastical prerogative.

By the same token, the language of servanthood cannot be used to sanctify the servitude of women or slaves. This is the other way, complementary to the first, that the language of service has been misused. When those who have been subjected in society ask for dignity and equal personhood, we say:

> The gospel exhorts us to humility. It even tells us to be slaves.
> Therefore the highest thing you can do is to accept your
> humiliated role. You will be rewarded in heaven.

In this way the socially revolutionary message of the gospel is evacuated and made into a rationale for maintaining a status quo of oppression.

Service or servanthood as the model of leadership has nothing to do with sanctifying dominance. But neither does it have anything to do with sanctifying the servitude of the oppressed. Jesus does not use the language of servanthood to idealize the role of women or slaves. Indeed the one time when he uses the term *serving* in a negative manner is when he is speaking to a woman, Martha. Martha's complaint against her sister Mary represents the woman conditioned to the traditional female role. Mary is the one who is out of place. Judaism did not believe that women were "called to the Torah." They were not supposed to study the Scriptures as disciples of the teacher—and to be a disciple was also, eventually, to become, oneself, a rabbi. Women were to stay in the kitchen and send their husbands and sons to the synagogue. Mary, in effect, was claiming her right to be an equal member in the circle of disciples. Martha wants Jesus to endorse the traditional role of women by putting Mary back "in her place." But instead Jesus rebukes Martha, not only for finding her only identity in this "woman's place," but also for using this "woman's place" to keep other women from growing:

But Martha was distracted with much serving; and she went to him and said, "Lord, do you not care that my sister has left me to serve alone? Tell her then to help me." But the Lord answered her, "Martha, Martha, you are anxious and troubled about many things; one thing is needful. Mary has chosen the better part which shall not be taken away from her."   (Luke 10:40–42)

How many sermons on this text have tried to do just that: to take away from Mary Jesus' justification of her claim to the "better part"! Jesus does not praise Mary and Martha equally. Instead he makes it clear that the kind of gospel he teaches calls women out of these traditional roles into equal membership in the circle of disciples. The kind of service he has in mind for these disciples, then, cannot be confused with the servitude of traditional roles of women and slaves "distracted with much serving," but is possible only on the other side of liberation from such roles. Service is possible only for the autonomous and empowered person who uses this power in a new way, not to subjugate but to empower others. This is service: a revolution in the very concept of leadership!

As we look in the writings of the developing church we see an increasing tendency to bury this liberating message, particularly as it applies to women. Paul reiterates the equality of men and women, slaves and free, Jew and Greek, *in Christ*! Paul himself probably understood this equality in Christ to be evidenced by the new roles of leadership women and slaves played in the Christian community, but he didn't want this equality within the church to be used to shake up social relations in society. He insisted that the traditional orders of obedience in the family and in the state were still intact within the present "era" of creation. Thus Paul lent himself to the identification of the headship of male over female, master over slave, with the "order of creation," even though he himself thought this order was temporary and would soon pass away with the return of Christ (see, for example, Rom. 13:11–12).

It was not long, however, before the post-Pauline church used Paul's authority to remove women from church leadership and to reaffirm the traditional subordination of women:

> Let a woman learn in silence with all submissiveness. I permit no woman to teach or to have authority over men; she is to keep silent.   (1 Tim. 2:11–12)

Likewise:

> Let all who are under the yoke of slavery regard their masters as worthy of all honor, . . . Those who have believing masters must not be disrespectful on the ground that they are brethren; rather they must serve all the better. . . . (1 Tim. 6:1–2)

The Christ-church relationship is made to sanctify a hierarchical relation of husband over wife, making the husband the Lord of the wife, as Christ is Lord of the church:

> For the husband is the head of the wife as Christ is the head of
> the church, his body, and is himself its Savior. As the church
> is subject to Christ, so let wives also be subject in everything
> to their husbands.   (Eph. 5:23)

The Christ-church, even the God-creature, relationship is
again modeled after worldly kingship and, in turn, used to
sanctify rulership of men over women. Taken literally, the
husband is seen as possessing divine prerogative over his
wife—which is idolatry! It was not long before the same
model of lord-subject, head—body, was applied to the relationship between leaders and people in the church. Ignatius
of Antioch, in a period contemporary with the later writings
of the New Testament, does not mind comparing himself
with God the Father and Christ as monarchical Lord of the
church. What has happened to that revolutionary model of
service suggested in the Gospels?

There is one alternative to this image of Jesus as the
supermasculinist "King of kings" which is popular among
Christian preachers. This is to speak of Jesus as androgyn-
ous. It is said that Jesus' power is gentleness and meekness.
Jesus integrates the "masculine" and "feminine" qualities
by this gentleness. The problem with this model of the
feminine Christ is very much like the problem of confusing
service with servitude. Femaleness is still identified in a
system of male dominance with qualities of submission.
Even worse, the whole Christian community is directed
toward roles of passivity in relationship to the power sys-
tems of society. The "gentle Jesus meek and mild" promotes
a pacified laity in relation to the dominance of the present
political and social order. The good Christian is one who
smiles a lot and doesn't rock the boat. Egoism and dominance are still identified with maleness, and femaleness with
submission. Males can play it out of both sides of this
dominance-submission model, but women are directed only
to auxiliary, supportive roles within this system of "com-

plementarity." Ruler-subject, clergy-laity, and husband-wife still continue as mutually reenforcing models of dominance and submission.

We need to rediscover the revolutionary potential of the concept of ministry suggested in the Gospel sayings. Service is not a code word for a new power trip, nor a sanctimonious way of justifying the servitude of the enslaved. It is a revolution that overthrows all these models of relationship. It means the self-emptying of alienated male power, even alienated divine power. Those who have set themselves up to use power to dominate others relinquish it to become servants. Who has ever seen those in power do this voluntarily? Never. Perhaps that is why God "himself" has to inaugurate this revolution by giving up the alienation of divine power that buttresses this worldly power. It is God who begins the *kenosis,* or emptying, of alienated power projected on the throne of heaven as the apotheosis of alienated male kingly power. It is God who becomes a servant, pulling out the foundations of all other kings and lords who use the divine as the model of hierarchy.

This emptying of God into service in the world, in turn, liberates those who have been oppressed. Women, slaves, are called out of their servitude to become equals—sisters and brothers in the community of the liberated humanity. It is the poor and the oppressed who must lead the way into the kingdom of God. It is in the *persona* of a woman that the church, the new Israel, proclaims its liberation: in her, God

> has scattered the proud in the imagination of their hearts,
> . . . put down the mighty from their thrones,
> and exalted those of low degree;
> . . . filled the hungry with good things,
> and the rich he has sent empty away. (Luke 1:51–53)

Those who have power must overthrow their own false

power by becoming the empowerers of the oppressed. They must identify themselves with servants, with those whom they have enslaved. Those who have been despised are seen as first in the community of the new humanity. Only by becoming one with their liberation do all of us, female and male, black and white, poor and rich, discover our own wholeness, in ourselves and with each other. This is the liberated and reconciled humanity which the gospel proclaims, but which we, the church, have yet to learn to believe and to fulfill.

Peggy Ann Way

Fools, Clowns, and Temptations

Isaiah 40:28–31; Romans 1:8–17*; Luke 24:1–12

The sermon this morning consists of simple reflections on fools, clowns, and their temptations—with an eye to liberation, and a centering on the nature and experience of God.

The sermon is, of course, my story, which illumines only as it may touch into your stories, too . . .

So come with me, and think yourselves of fools, clowns, and temptations.

Fools

I was far into my ministries—too far to step back—before I recognized the intrinsic foolishness of Christian ministry. I kept seeing things that others did not seem to see, and saying what were not welcome words, and making offerings that could not be received. Through it all, I kept feeling the love of caring and the pain of justice unrealized. And I kept living. . . .

I remember, from my ministries in relation to human sexuality, and some of you may share such memories, too—

I remember the first homophile organizations in Chicago,

---

*In verse 13, "brethren" became "brothers" and "sisters," and in verse 15, it was read as "Hyde Park," the community in which the sermon was given.

and my presence among the people who were there, and my discovery that many of them had pseudonyms because they did not dare let people know their names. And I remember how foolish I thought it that these, God's people, could not have their own names. And I remember my first TV interviews with persons who were homosexual, and how they had to appear in shadow, and how foolish I thought it that they could not have faces. I remember . . . only ten years ago!

I remember being asked to speak to women's groups in churches about how I could justify being in ministry when I had children . . . and I remember—and still hear about—women being interviewed by pulpit committees or denominational committees and being asked nothing about their theologies, only about various aspects of their sexuality. And I remember thinking . . . how foolish . . .

I remember always, through the gifts of travel that I have received in my ministries, the countless numbers of women and of homosexual persons that I have been blessed to know . . . who have shared with me their depths of religious experience and their sense of call, their Christian commitments and love of service . . . and I have thought: how foolish, that we have trouble receiving such gifts.

Such memories flow through mixtures of smiles and tears, pathos and joy, anger and gentleness . . . and come together in such simple ways of foolish seeing as these:

The absurdity of a church or Christian community organized around sexuality—whether women/men, or gay/straight, or celibate/not celibate—centering its key valuations and issuing its clearest statements around matters of sex;
the absurdity of a church organization that has, as its

64943

determinative principles of membership and access to leadership, nothing of greater importance than sexual organs or sexual orientations;

and most absurd of all: the attempt of the church to control God by limiting God's freedom to work through and call any of those created in the image and the spirit . . . to limit God's choice to ours, with our primary criterion being that of sexuality, so that one may be ordained without a commitment to justice, but not without properly sanctioned sexuality.

This is not to say that the church has nothing to say about matters of human sexuality—for indeed it does—but we must look to that on another day. Today we are merely to share in experiences of being the fool . . . of seeing what seems so clear, of speaking what appears so true, of offering what seems so positive—the gifts of those of God's people who would present themselves as colleagues in the tasks of care and justice.

What Means It, Then, to Be the Fool?

First, it is a way of seeing, which may not be as others see. It means a way of speaking about what is seen—as the women spoke their idle tales which turned out to be about the resurrection. It means being responded to and treated as a speaker of idle tales. It means having enough faith and trust to hear the idle tales spoken to you and not to reject them out of hand because they are "only" spoken by women.

Thus the fool may speak what others understand as idle tales, and it is probable that we all do this whenever we speak of the gospel. The fool will also listen to the idle tales of others—the poor, the dispossessed, the outsider. For the fool doesn't need to be afraid, but can let in the idle tales, because . . .

Second, the fool knows that she or he is in for the long haul. The gospel commitment is not a commitment to a problem to be resolved, but to an understanding of the nature of human existence that is to be ongoingly lived. It is a commitment to caring and justice that goes on from generation to generation, even unto the ends of the earth. And from this knowledge, the fool gets her or his own style of naive courage and does not leave the battle when issues are not neatly resolved.

Third, the fool always points beyond her- or himself. The women were not telling of the resurrection for their own glory—but that a truth might be stated. For the true fool is always the fool for Christ. Not all tales are about resurrections, you see, and when we get to temptations we will suggest how we can tell the difference.

But for now we affirm that the experience of being the fool is intrinsic and not accidental to Christian ministry, whether one is lay or ordained. Perhaps this is clearest when one is part of a liberation movement, but surely it is a fully human experience. Have you not felt the fool, as part of a liberation movement or as part of *your* particular minority? Have you not had a vision of family life that is not shared by your spouse or children—or parents—and spoken of it, and not been heard? Have you not spoken foolishly in your parish? At times of absurdity, have you not sometimes spoken of meaning—and been looked at as the fool?

Being the fool is very similar to the experience of being a Christian—of looking at the world with eyes of faith, of letting go guarantee and control, of listening to those from whom others turn away. And it means not only listening, but sharing with them and working together. It is celebrating in the midst of chaos and living in a stream of existence with continual crises where life never becomes "neat," and it is trying to share what is important with others and not being heard. It is to keep on living, seeing, caring, being just, IN SPITE OF . . . the latter, perhaps, is the most foolish of all.

Clowns

Now what of clowns? The clown, too, is an image to sustain those of us who would identify ourselves with Christian ministry. I will share three clown images with you. A Dutch pastoral theologian, Heije Faber, has lifted up the first image of the clown that sustains me in my foolish ministries.

If the clown is not present, the circus is not whole! Yet the clown has no skills at which people gasp like those of the trapeze artist . . . has no marketable product which you buy, like tickets or popcorn . . . has no neat, organizing function or office like the owner of the circus. . . . has no animal that has been trained to perform . . .

In fact, the clown is clumsy, fails, is absurd, is laughed at—or is it laughed with? The clown gets the sympathy and the empathy, catches us into feelings of ambiguity of life, smiles at failure. Primarily, perhaps, the clown puts things in perspective, the many sides of life. There, in the midst of those accomplishing great feats, sometimes with danger, in the middle of those acting with great competence and skill, sits the clown, the human, the ordinary. Slightly antisocial, perhaps, with a feel for the fringes, and, in Faber's words, "a kind of irresponsibility, carelessness, and inner freedom; ability to share suffering, compassion, and humanity . . . a pattern of life of another order, on another wave length."

Have you not sometimes felt that way? On another wave length? Seeing things differently? Being laughed at? Trying to keep things in perspective? And with what roots or cour-

age or aplomb do you keep with it? You, fool. You, clown.
But let me share a second image, this one from a poet, e. e.
cummings. Think of your own images, your own ministries,
your own moments from within the human circus . . .

one winter afternoon

(at the magical hour
when is becomes if)

a bespangled clown
standing on eighth street
handed me a flower.

Nobody,it's safe
to say,observed him but

myself;and why?because

without any doubt he was
whatever(first and last)

mostpeople fear most:
a mystery for which i've
no word except alive

—that is,completely alert
and miraculously whole;

with not merely a mind and a heart

but unquestionably a soul—
by no means funereally hilarious

(or otherwise democratic)
but essentially poetic
or ethereally serious:

a fine not a coarse clown
(no mob,but a person)

and while never saying a word

who was anything but dumb;
since the silence of him

self sang like a bird.
Mostpeople have been heard
screaming for international

measures that render hell rational
—i thank heaven somebody's crazy

enough to give me a daisy*

Do you ever feel like that? Do you sometimes feel like a
clown when making offerings to others? When telling idle
tales, being present with, standing in the midst of a complex
culture that you and I can't control but that we continually
try at least to order . . . and sometimes, within it, just for a
moment, let ourselves be . . . the clown?

Now Harvey Cox's clown, our third image, is different—a
bit more radical, perhaps, but still . . . quite strange.

ON CHRIST THE CLOWN

Stop that man!
The painted juggler with the idiotic grin,
And all his motley gaggle
Of harlequins, fat ladies and sword swallowers.
They're all fakes, I think.
At least they're unwelcome intruders into our well-calibrated,
Surprise-free universe.
We had read that he was dead.
Can't believe anything you read these days, but we did,
Despite the lilies and anthems and all.
Oh, we knew our noses were itching for something,
With all the beads and mantras and incense.
But he was so gray and unavailable.
Embalmed by church and state. To be viewed on high unfestive
occasions.
Is the minstrel really back? That inept troubadour whose unpolitic
legerdemain
Finally got him lynched

E. E. Cummings, "one winter afternoon," no. 30, from "73 Poems." Copyright
1960 by E. E. Cummings. Reprinted from his volume *Complete Poems 1913-1962*
by permission of Harcourt Brace Jovanovich, Inc.

By the imperial security forces?
Back? Not a chance. Though there are these funny rumors,
But they come from the usual unreliable sources: spooked-out
undependable
People, notorious liars. Ladies of shady repute. Sleight-of-hand
artists.
They let on he lives, like love and laughter and man's eternal
gullibility.
But who can believe people like them?
Children do, and fools. Maybe a few meter maids.
But who else?
Who else?*

Temptations

If there are fools and Fools—and clowns and Clowns—
and illusions and a resurrection: how are we to tell the
difference? I leave you with the ongoing question, and a few
clues to guide . . .

First, the fool for Christ—or she who speaks about the
resurrection—is quite clear that she is not God. The fool or
the clown in the spirit of this sermon, says very clearly: I AM
NOT GOD. It is my own belief to speak of God as man,
woman, gay, black, red . . . but it symbolizes the bankruptcy
of theology and of religious experience. When we see differently, live on another wavelength, we seek to offer perspectives on existence broader and deeper than our own. The fool
for Christ points beyond herself—by definition. And the
Clown in the Human Circus puts existence in a perspective
that transcends his own.

Second, by pointing beyond self or putting events in perspective, the fool does not make the mistake that James
Gustafson, in his ethical probings, refers to as "thematic
unitarianism." It is to point to dimensionality, complexity,
differing wavelengths that the fool speaks and the clown

---

*Harvey Cox, *Seduction of the Spirit* (New York: Simon and Schuster, 1973),
p. 330. Used with permission.

lives, and not to look at everything through only one point of view. Even, for me, sexism. Even racism, or social class, or economics. Even my favorite. Even yours. We are called to dimensional perspectives on sin and salvation, life and death, sex and poverty, peace and organizing, social class and developmental psychology . . . a way of seeing that can take in anything and not be totally encompassed by any one of them.

And when we act the fool or clown, we must be reminded that sometimes that is a luxury. While changing a welfare system, somebody must get the checks out on time. The garbage needs picking up, ordinary living goes on, and not all are freed or called to see the foolishness and be the clown—always a part of, but always, too, apart from . . .

And third, a clue to authentic fooldom or clowndom is the recognition of being there for the long haul. Some idle tales are of short-term projects, but the fools tell of a way of life, an understanding of history, an intrinsic identification of pain with human existence and of joy in spite of its possibilities. It is, always, a living of caring and justice throughout a lifetime, with the living of that style its own integrity and truth.

> Fools, Clowns, Temptations. Think on these things.
> One of my Jesuit friends wrote something similar
>   on his invitations to his ordination:
>> We are simply asked
>> to make gentle
>> our bruised world
>> to tame its savageness
>> to be compassionate of all
>> including oneself
>> then, with the time left over
>> to repeat the ancient tale
>> and go the way
>> of God's foolish ones.
> For have you not heard? have you not known?

The Lord is the everlasting God . . . the Creator . . .
And we who wait on the Lord will renew our strength.
She will rise up on wings like eagles!
He will walk and not grow weary!
We will run and not faint!

Dorothee Soelle

The Children of Soweto

Soweto is an abbreviation for *South Western To*wnships; the name applies to the segregated black townships under the control of the Johannesburg City Council. Soweto is the fifth largest city in Africa, south of the Sahara, a home of nearly a million blacks, the overwhelming majority of them living in austere four-roomed houses with neither electricity nor water.

The parents of school children in this area are in the humiliating position of lacking the means to meet the minimal demands of their children for school fees and books, school uniforms and blouses. Whites have free education; only blacks have to pay. The characteristics of the system of Bantu education are: overcrowded classrooms, lack of teachers, poorly educated teachers, an acute shortage of secondary schools, and an alarmingly high drop-out rate at all levels. Bantu education is designed to deny blacks any role in society other than that of a worker and servant.

On 16 June 1976, about 15,000 Soweto school children marched through the township in protest against the mandatory use of the Afrikaans language as a medium of instruction in black schools. The government had ordered that mathematics, history, and geography be taught in Afrikaans, a language which is alien to black students as well as to their teachers. We Are Not Boers, and, Afrikaans: The Language of the Oppressor, were slogans written on the placards carried by the children. They had been on strike against the

Bantu education directive for five weeks by boycotting classes. According to eyewitnesses, the demonstration, which was "entirely a children's affair," was peaceful until a tear-gas shell fired by one of a contingent of policemen set the day ablaze. The children started throwing stones and other light missiles as a result. The police retaliated by firing shots at the children who were right in front. These children were aged between eight and ten years; the first shots landed on a boy about ten years old. One witness reported: "What the police did, was to set a dog on a child. The dog bit the child and the students naturally got hold of the dog to protect the child, and as they did that this particular policeman fired the first shots at this child, who died on the spot. That is how the dog got killed and that is how they provoked about 15,000 school children." The children were then attacking any white in the black townships and burning all vehicles bearing the Westrand Administration Boarding markings. At that stage the only passport to safety was the "black solidarity" sign. Instances were reported of whites who were left untouched after they had shown the solidarity sign. According to official South African Government figures, 325 people have been killed, three of whom were white. Thousands have been injured and hundreds arrested under the Riotous Assemblies Act and the Internal Security Act. Black leaders, however, touring the country, estimate that as many as one thousand blacks have been killed.

Close your eyes. Remember the photos you probably have seen. Recall their slogans: Our Teachers Can't Teach in Afrikaans and Do Not Force Afrikaans Down Our Throats. Look in their faces; listen to their cry; see their clenched fists. Remember the children of Soweto; remember their ages running from eight to eighteen: remember the eights, the nines, the tens, the elevens, the twelves . . . remember the school children and the drop-outs. Remember the parentless and those who had to educate their parents. Remember your own childhood; remember the humiliations you experienced, the tears you wept, the bitterness you felt when you first saw injustice triumphing. Remember how they put you down and how you swallowed it.

Remember how you and I and everybody here were taught to learn the language of the oppressor; to talk Afrikaans and Nazi German and Advertisement language; and remember how well we learned it.

Remember the children of Soweto. There was a little black boy standing on one side of a street in Soweto. He had a rock in his hand. On the other side of the street there were policemen with guns. A reporter standing nearby asked the boy, "Are you going to throw the rock?" The boy said, "Yes." The reporter said, "They will kill you." And the boy responded, "They may kill me, but I am right." Remember the children of Soweto.

> And it shall come to pass afterward,
>   that I will pour out my spirit on all flesh;
> your sons and your daughters shall prophesy,
>   your old men shall dream dreams,
>   and your young men shall see visions.
> Even upon the menservants and maidservants
>   in those days, I will pour out my spirit.

"And I will give portents in the heavens and on the earth, blood and fire and columns of smoke. The sun shall be turned to darkness, and the moon to blood, before the great and terrible day of the Lord comes."   (Joel 2:28–31)

What can the children of Soweto teach us?

The uniqueness of the situation is that the children decided to take the matter of Afrikaans into their own hands after their parents had taken it lightly. It seems to have opened the eyes of most parents that children who appear to be more vocal on the apartheid issue will take the lead if need be.

Comments by the parents such as, "Our children have shown us the lead," and "Shame, that our children had to die for us in the struggle," are common in the townships.

The voiceless have found a voice. God pours his Spirit upon sons and daughters, upon slaves and slavegirls. When Jesus called children to him, his disciples rebuked them, but Jesus said, "Do not try to stop them: for the kingdom of heaven belongs to such as these" (Matt. 19:14). We have often listened to this story with a sentimental feeling; let's now hear it in a revolutionary sense. Sentimentality belongs to the language of the oppressor; the kingdom of heaven belongs to the children of Soweto.

When we sat together to prepare this worship service, Linda mentioned that she felt a lack of praising the Lord. I felt uncomfortable and impatient with that. Should we praise the Lord when 325 people, most of them children, are murdered? Can we praise the Lord in the time of oppression, when we cry for peace, but there is no peace? But when I reflected more on this question of praising the Lord, I found out that Linda was right, and my understanding of praise was only on the surface. Preparing a service together means growing together.

So let us praise the Lord for the children of Soweto. Let us praise the Lord who gave us new teachers; let us praise the Lord for the children who are teaching us truth and courage. These are the gifts of the Spirit; the Spirit tells us the truth and she encourages us. The children told the truth with rocks and their people were encouraged. Praise the Lord for the children of Soweto. Praise the Lord for what is in us: our hate against the system which has to murder children in order to maintain domination and profits. Praise the Lord for what is in us: our despair, our feeling of powerlessness, and our solidarity and hope. Praise the Lord for the language, that we begin to unlearn the Afrikaans of the oppressor and begin to learn the language of the liberator. Praise the Lord for the children of Soweto. Amen.

Beatriz Melano Couch

Suffering and Hope

1 Peter: 1:1–7, 4:12–19

James, 1 and 2 Peter, John, and Jude are called the catholic epistles because they were written for all the Christians of their time. In this they are different from most of the epistles of Paul, because he always writes to particular persons or churches or friends he has known. The church fathers call these epistles universal or catholic, precisely because they were directed to all Christians. The main topic in James is works; in John, love; in Jude, pure faith; and in Peter, hope. The basic question of the Epistle of Peter is: What is the meaning of Christian hope in a non-Christian world where Christians are afflicted, confused, bewildered, and dispersed throughout all Asia Minor?

These Christians were, literally speaking, refugees or exiles just as the epistle calls them. They were converted Jews dispersed in the world outside Palestine. The text tells us that they were chosen and destined by God himself, sanctified by the Holy Spirit, and that their mission was obedience to Jesus Christ.

Today, we live in a world where there are many more exiles or refugees than perhaps in any other time of history. Millions are exiles for political or religious reasons, or both. Those scattered and persecuted Christians who wander all over the earth are not alone in their suffering of exile and persecution; they belong to us and we belong to them, because we are all part of the household of the Lord. Their suffering is our suffering, and their hope our hope. This is the meaning of oneness in Christ, of being in one single body no matter how we may be separated by geographical distance. The Leitmotiv of Peter's letter takes on new meaning and an unprecedented urgency, precisely because of this painful experience of the people of God in our day.

I would like to interpret this text, relating it to our experience in Latin America. Consider these reflections as our letter to you, dear sisters and brothers in the northern hemisphere. Our struggle, our suffering and hope are our gift to you in the love that makes us one.

First, we will ask the text three questions: Where is hope rooted? What is its sustaining element? What is this hope after all? And then we will continue to ask: Of what kind of suffering does Peter speak? What does it mean to partake of Christ's sufferings in our world?

Where is hope rooted? *Hope is rooted in praise.* "Blessed be the God and Father of our Lord Jesus Christ!" (1 Pet. 1:3). Blessing God in the midst of exile and in the midst of suffering is the initial step toward a concrete understanding of the meaning of Christian hope. This verse acknowledges God's merciful initiative. God who loved us first . . . by his great mercy.

What is the sustaining element in this hope? Where is it centered? *It is centered in the resurrection;* this event generates hope: ". . . born anew to a living hope through the resurrection of Jesus Christ from the dead" (1:3). Is it not true that our hopes and our despairs are generated in facts and in events, not in ideas or in concepts?

For example, when a child is born into a family who has eagerly waited for a child, the very event of its birth generates joy and hope. How many hopes for the future of a new human being wanted and loved! It is a gift to all of humanity. On the contrary, when a doctor comes out of an operating room and says, "We have done everything we could; there is nothing more we can do," this very fact creates pain and despair. Things that *happen* and in which we participate actively in one way or another generate hope or despair. Hope is not an idea but a response to an event. It is something that happens within us that is reflected in our emotions, attitudes, perspectives about the fundamental issues of life.

What does it mean that the event of the resurrection of Christ is the center of all hope? It means that Christ's lordship is over all history and creation and that salvation (1:5) gives meaning to history, gives meaning to life—to personal, individual life and to communal life. History is not cyclical. We are no longer wanderers in a desert with no road ahead, nor are we alone in our struggle to survive as humans. Because Christ is Lord over all, because he has conquered sin and death, because he came to initiate the new era—the era of the kingdom, the human pilgrimage acquires a new sense and direction.

What is this hope? Is it a feeling, a concept, an idea, an illusion, a projection, a desire, a dream, an experience, a human wish? No, it is a living, active reality (1:3–4). It is a new creation, a new possibility of life "born anew to a living hope," or "born again into a life full of hope" (Phillips). It is a gift, an inheritance. There are three adjectives in the Revised Standard Version to qualify this gift: "imperishable," in a world where nothing lasts too long; "undefiled," in a world where everything is prostituted; and "unfading," in a world where everything fades and disappears. In the New English Bible, instead of three adjectives we have three verbs to describe the nature of this inheritance: it is "one that nothing can destroy or spoil or wither." In the Phillips translation, this new hope which is a gift and a perfect inheritance is "beyond the reach of change and decay." This hope is in nothing less than God's power. It is a hope based on the reality of the power of God at work; it is not a mere human wish; it is a power that guards and saves (1:5).

Hope is generated, initiated, and grows, continues, develops, is nurtured precisely by the power of God at work. Otherwise, it fades and is no longer hope but a dim illusion with no consistency. What gives consistency to our hope is Christ himself. Therefore, it is a living hope in a living Christ. That is why a hope that is centered in the resurrection is a living presence and a living power. If the Easter message is: Jesus Christ Is Alive, the message of Christian hope is also Jesus Christ Lives Today!

To whom does this message speak? Does it speak to those who are well-established in today's world? To those who are well-situated politically, who are socially and economically satisfied? Does it speak to those who have little or nothing to hope for? If I am not unemployed, I do not need to hope for a job. If I am not sick, I do not need to hope for health. If I am not in prison, I do not need to hope for freedom. If I am not lonely, I do not need to hope for love and friends. If I am not oppressed, I will not hope for deliverance. Only to those who sense their deep need does hope speak.

Hope speaks in the midst of our emptiness, in the midst of our despair, futility, loneliness, oppression. That is why true hope grows and develops in the midst of suffering. This is the reason why after this immense confession of hope, this symphony of hope, Peter immediately, with the word *rejoice*, introduces the theme of suffering and trial. Suffering, without hope, produces anger and hate and rejection, but suffering nurtured by the living hope can create love, reconciliation, new vision, new life, new possibilities of humanity.

The second Leitmotiv of this letter is the theme of suffering. Peter speaks of two different kinds of suffering and the difference is highly important. There is a kind of suffering which is the by-product of sin, malice, selfishness, egotism.

It is described thus: "If you suffer, it must not be for murder, theft, or sorcery, not for infringing the rights of others" (4:15, NEB). There is a lot of unnecessary pain in the world which is the product of human brokenness or sin: the agony produced here several months ago by the death of a young boy poisoned by his own companions in a gang addicted to drugs; the pathological drive to destroy ourselves and others by reducing people to mere objects to be used and manipulated—racially, sexually, politically, economically; the long-lasting, painful memory in an innocent child's soul after being brutally attacked by a mob bent on stealing a bicycle; the institutionalized violence that is rooted in the very structures of an unjust society which causes, for three-fourths of the world's population, subhuman living conditions. All of these types of suffering are the consequence of human sin and selfishness.

But there are other kinds of suffering which are the outcome of our service to Christ. Last Christmas Eve an older priest was attacked as he was going to say mass. As a consequence of this act of violence, a few hours later he died in a hospital in the city of Cordoba, a holiday-resort place about 800 miles from the city of Buenos Aires. His only "sin" was that he had identified with the oppressed, the poor, and the underprivileged. He had no affiliations with any political parties, nor did he belong to a guerrilla group. It can be a very dangerous thing to take the message of deliverance seriously.

What does Peter call those Christians who are suffering for Christ's sake? He calls them "beloved," "dear friends of mine," "my dear friends." He addresses them affectionately. He shares their pain. If Christ's love abides in us, we cannot but share the pain of those who suffer along the road of faithfulness to a Lord of justice and love.

Peter, after addressing affectionately those exiled Christians who were going through trials for their faith, continues admonishing them by saying, "Do not be surprised at the fiery ordeal which comes upon you . . ." (4:12). "Think it not strange"; "I beg you not to be unduly alarmed"; "Do not be bewildered," are different versions of this same text. They were not to behave as though this were something extraordinary, or an unusual experience. It is not something unusual or extraordinary. It is exactly what happens to Christians when they take God's word seriously—when they obey literally the commandment to release the captives, setting people free from oppression, feeding the hungry, clothing the naked, visiting those in jail, proclaiming the acceptable year of the Lord. The fiery ordeal is nothing more and nothing less than to share in Christ's suffering as the Christian community bears faithful witness to him in a hostile world.

Peter had every right to speak because "he knew from personal experience what it is to be hunted by the secret police, to suffer imprisonment for his faith, to live the precarious life of the persecuted."*

This fiery ordeal is a reality in our time. Many suffer—as Christians and as human beings—intimidation, imprisonment, torture, exile, martyrdom, concentration camps. And all these bring vividly to mind similar violence which runs all through the pages of the New Testament. The faithful were always persecuted. During the first three centuries of the Christian era, there were ten persecutions. The same happened again under the Nazi regime, and today under the dictatorships of the extreme right and left. So we are not to be surprised. Christ was crucified. Then as now the establishment could not tolerate him.

The cross was the world's judgment on Christ. There will always be a difference between Christ's ways and the

---

*The Interpreter's Bible, 12 vols. (Nashville: Abingdon Press, 1957), 3:143.

world's ways. On the contrary, think it strange if we are not persecuted in our own day. "For Christians to be so safely conformed to the world and its course of living that they run into no trouble at all may well be an indication that they have de-natured their way of life of its radical, world-judging, world-changing spirit, . . . or perhaps the New Testament conception of the Christ has been conveniently toned down, maybe even lost through a dangerous ignorance of the nature of Christianity. Christ is no serviceable addendum to human life; he is the radical center to which life must be reconciled and conformed."*

But for the Christian, ordeal, trial, and suffering should not be regarded as tragedy. There is no tragedy in God's economy, in God's plan. Nothing comes by chance, nothing that happens is useless or lost.

Some months ago a Protestant pastor in a Latin-American country was taken to prison with no charge against him. He did not belong to any political party, he did not belong to any "subversive" group; he was suspect only for the mere fact of being a pastor. On the same day, a priest, a judge, a doctor, and some other people were taken to jail too, apparently a preventive measure, since the President was going to appear in town the next day. For five days and five nights the pastor was made to stand with his hands against the wall, and was beaten every time he collapsed of exhaustion. Some of the members of his congregation went to his home to comfort his young wife and his children, and the word soon got around that anyone who went to the manse would also be taken to jail peremptorily with no charges. Some people stayed away from the manse and the church, but others, knowing that they would be taken to jail, went to console the wife. Fifteen days later, when they were all released—with no explanation

---

*Ibid.

of any sort, no trial, no possibility of defense—that small congregation, in a very small Latin-American village, worshipped. There were no words of bitterness against anyone; there was no defense, personal or communal; there was no spirit of aggression or violence against the injustice inflicted and suffered. A rather small group of people who were united through suffering, gathered to worship united in community, in mission, and in destiny, and there was joy and praise. Mutual sharing of pain creates an understanding fellowship. Christ enters into our ordeals more profoundly than we can ever enter into his. Peter writes out of this experience. And the church in Latin America is also speaking out of this experience. Many testify to the fact that there is no greater joy than partaking in Christ's purposes and participating in his love. This means sharing the cross in a very concrete way with others and with a Lord who is ahead of us and is also our rear guard. This is a source of true hope, a hope that is no longer a concept that one emits from behind a desk in a comfortable study, but a hope that is born from the experience of sharing together in the Lord's purposes in our time.

Let me finish with two quotations from two letters I have recently received. One of them is from Seoul, Korea, and the other one from a Latin-American country. In both places, Christians and non-Christians are persecuted when they denounce the injustices of a system of oppression and extremely cruel repression. "Over and over again we have witnessed a deepened faith and a renewed vigor of those persons of true faith and deep conscience who have been through the experience of arrest, sham trials, and imprisonment. In one case we know of, the children of a man arrested made a thank offering in their church the Sunday after his incarceration saying that they were thankful to God for having given them a father of whom they could be so proud." And from Latin America: ". . . 'X' is handling a few cases for people who were detained by the forces of order and held prisoners under very questionable circumstances. This kind of thing has happened enough to be cause for alarm. Why do people always have to go from one extreme to the other? Is there nowhere a real passion for justice?"

If we are going to take very seriously the message of the Bible: the releasing of captives, the giving of sight to the blind, liberty to the oppressed, and the proclamation and acts of the acceptable year of the Lord; if we are going to try to obey the word of the prophets and of Jesus Christ and the testimony of the early church, we are going to run into trouble. We are going to be involved in Christ's work, which is world-judging, world-condemning, world-transforming. This may bring to us not only unpopularity among our friends, family, and churches, but probably some things that are more costly. So, we should not enter into discipleship unless we are willing to pay the price, to pay the cost— avoiding all martyr complexes, all masochism, and all messianism—with the spirit of the joy which is grounded on the promises of God himself. Not only on the promises written in the Bible, but the promises of many Christians "written" in their experience of a living hope which is born from an encounter with a living God and with a whole host of witnesses in the Christian community through the centuries and around the world today.

> If you do away with the yoke,
> the clenched fist, the wicked word,
> if you give your bread to the hungry,
> and relief to the oppressed,
>
> your light will rise in the darkness,
> and your shadows become like noon.
> Yahweh will always guide you,
> giving you relief in desert places.

He will give strength to your bones
and you shall be like a watered garden,
like a spring of water
whose waters never run dry.

(Isa. 58:9–11 JB)

Helen Gray Crotwell

Broken Community

Acts 1:8-26

THE SEVENTH SUNDAY OF EASTER

We tell our stories as we tell about our communities. We tell who we are as we talk about our communities—our supporting communities, our nurturing communities, our judging communities, our broken, shattered, painful communities. Next Sunday many will be celebrating the birthday of the church, one of our primary Christian communities. Notice that our biblical story begins with community in the garden of Eden, soon broken, and ends with the promise of a new community, a new Jerusalem where every tear will be wiped away, and where there will be no death, no mourning, no pain. In between this beginning and this end is the record of people living with broken community, breaking community, shaping community, forming new community.

Jesus was in community—moving from one community to another, standing over against, supporting, breaking, changing, healing, comforting in community, and choosing a community of people to work with him, to continue his ministry, after he was gone. No matter how many times I read the Luke/Acts story I am amazed at the description of this community of people Jesus chose. For we have a story of a very ordinary band of followers—including a betrayer, a doubter, a denier, weak people, people who could not even stay awake with Jesus during his last night. There were tempestuous people—one flew into rage, even cutting off an ear—

124

but when Jesus was arrested, they all deserted him and ran from him, leaving him alone. When the women told them that Jesus was not dead, this bunch responded, "Nonsense."

Surely there were better people, more dependable people, Jesus could have chosen. Surely he could have used his miraculous power to give them more strength and courage. What a base for the foundation of the church! But here lies our hope. For God's action is not, and Jesus' ministry was not, dependent on people who were, who are, infallible; on people who did not, who do not make mistakes, or doubt, or get angry.

So much of the biblical story is the story of survival in spite of—or perhaps even because of—broken community, shattered dreams. This is the word we need to hear, for this is where we are living our lives—in broken communities, with shattered hope. But this is a hard word for us to hear, for we are anxious people, as individuals and as communities. We want certainty, security, success immediately. We have a difficult time living with our human limitations, our uncertainties, our ambiguities, our broken communities.

Our awareness of our human limitation is made more acute with our present emphasis on developing human potential, certainly an important concern, because most all of us have many dormant resources and possibilities which need to be developed. But the encouragement to develop our potential to its fullest can be destructive when it is translated, "You can do anything. There can be a perfect community, a perfect job, a perfect marriage, a perfect relationship." We aren't prepared when our life doesn't develop as we had planned. We have difficulty accepting broken community, shattered dreams, and we often destroy the existing possibility for community by searching for that ideal job, ideal marriage, ideal community, by not accepting our human limitations.

Now one of the important words that comes to us in our
Judeo-Christian heritage—one of the words we find recorded
between the story of our moving out of the community where
we had no knowledge of good and evil, and the story of our
hope of a new heaven and new earth where there will be no
pain—is the word, "This is the way life is. This is the way life
is given to us. This is what it means to be human." Much of
our life will be lived in broken communities, in breaking
communities, in moving out of bondage, out of Egypt into
the promised land. We must learn to live with this movement; we must learn to live as we break communities which
oppress us; we must learn to live with disappointment, denial, betrayal, shattered hopes. The word which comes to us
is not only, "This is what life is like," but is also, "We can
live in this place," because we know that God has not—will
not—does not—abandon us. The promise is: we can meet
God in this broken community, in this breaking of community. In fact this may be where we will be most aware of
God's presence: in our broken communities, in our moving
from communities of bondage, from Egypt toward the promised land. In meeting God here we are able to bless that
which we leave—so that we are not bound, chained to our
past, to our bondage, to our broken communities, to our
failures.

Look again at the New Testament lesson. Jesus had de-
parted. His followers had been promised that they would be
given power when the spirit came to them. There they were,
a broken community—Judas had betrayed them when he
betrayed Jesus. There they were, a weak community—
people who had deserted Jesus when things got tough, leaving him so alone he wondered even if God had forsaken him.
There they were, a broken community. Jesus had left them,
and they had not yet received the promised Spirit. But they
had gathered and were waiting. There is almost something

humorous about the scene. Imagine the people standing around with their eyes fixed to the sky waiting for Jesus to return, when two men appeared and asked them what they were doing standing there. I'm never quite sure why I'm always amused at this. I guess I wonder how long they would have stood there waiting had the two men not appeared and asked the question.

Now, we read this story from our perspective, 2000 years later. We know how it comes out, and forget that it must have been difficult for Jesus' followers to face their broken community. They had given up everything to follow Jesus, and then their community had fallen apart. We know that even when the group reassembled, and after they knew they had been given the power they had been promised, they had to keep living with broken dreams, unrealized expectations, and broken communities. They had been certain that Jesus was going to usher in God's kingdom in their lifetime, but he didn't do it. There were still death, and tears, and oppression, and betrayals, and denials. We can say the Bible really is the story of people surviving broken dreams, unrealized expectations, broken community, betrayal; not just surviving, but living, and learning to recognize God's presence in the midst of all the brokenness.

This is still our story, this is where we are still living. There is no person here who does not know about such brokenness firsthand. Look at a few of the broken communities we experience. First, we all know the pain of separation that comes when people graduate, or change jobs, when children leave home, when old people die. We feel sadness and grief. But we anticipate this type of broken community, we expect it, and in some sense, we plan for the separation.

There is another kind of broken community which is more difficult for us—the one we did not anticipate or choose. We have all experienced the unexpected death of people we love who die before they have fully lived. We grieve over our loss for a long time. Community broken by tragic death is difficult for us to understand. We have all been touched directly or indirectly by such meaningless tragedies.

Many of us, perhaps most of us, also know the pain and anguish and despair which comes when the community of the family, is broken . . . by unfaithfulness, betrayal, separation, or divorce. Even when this seems the only option, it is still painful and agonizing for all persons involved. The deep grief which is caused by the shattering of a family extends beyond the limits of family to the friends, to all who love them.

There is another kind of broken community which can be just as painful, even though it is chosen. A decision may be made by some people or by a group to break community. An example is the broken community many blacks and whites feel—especially those who were involved in the early civil rights movement. In their movement out of bondage, out of Egypt, towards liberation, blacks had to assume responsibility for the leadership in their struggle to be free, which meant a separation from some of their white brothers and sisters who had been working with them. Some community had to be broken as blacks assumed leadership. This was a painful separation, for many blacks and whites. And we rejoice at the signs of hope we now see, blacks and whites working together to eliminate all forms of oppression and injustice.

As women struggle to move out of bondage, out of Egypt to the promised land, there is breaking—or changing—of communities which restrict us or limit our growth as persons. We know some of the dangers we face—one being that we may dehumanize other men and women as we fight against our own dehumanization. We know this involves pain for us and much pain for many men. And sometimes, just as the Israelites said to Moses: "We'd rather have stayed in Egypt where at least we had plenty to eat. What does it mean to be out of bondage, out here in the wilderness, where we are all going to starve to death?" Or as Carole Etzler wrote in a song, "Sometimes I wish my eyes hadn't been opened; sometimes I wish I could no longer see all of the pain and the hurt and the longing of my sisters and me as we try to be free." It is painful, but it is important for all of us, men and women, to move out of Egypt toward the promised land where there is no Jew nor Greek, slave nor free, male nor female.

What is the word that comes to us out of our biblical faith when we are living with the pain of broken community, when we are facing the possibility of breaking community? It's helpful to be reminded that life comes to us with pain. To be human means to love and hate, laugh and cry, hurt and be hurt. Such pain and joy, agony and ecstasy is part of the gift of freedom, of being people who are given responsibility, choices, decisions. We do not live in the garden of Eden. Sometimes our communities will be broken, our plans will be shattered, our faith and hope will be faint and weak. Sometimes we can understand, accept, claim our responsibility for intentionally or unintentionally breaking community. But sometimes there is no understanding—only pain and hurt and grief; and we can get trapped and feed on our hurt and grief and be afraid to move out.

This spring a recent Duke graduate—whose future lay before, whose dreams, hopes, and potential were still growing and developing—was killed, murdered. Our community was broken, shattered, numb. In the memorial service for her, Bob Young said: "Let's not give any dignity to this tragic, inhuman act by saying that there is meaning in it. Let's face both the mystery and the meaninglessness of it all, accept it, fight it, curse it, endure it, live with it—but not make it good. There is no meaning here, nothing good in what happened. Here is the ultimate expression of the depravity of one human mind as it destroys another. This is sheer tragedy . . . our hope lies in our trust in God." And in the assurance we get from Paul's words that nothing can separate us from God's love—nothing in life or death has that power.

What is the word which comes to us when we face the anxiety and fear of intentionally breaking, or fracturing a community which we believe must be enlarged, expanded, made more human or more inclusive? We are supported when we remember that changing community is what much of the gospel is about. This is what Jesus was talking about when he read from Isaiah, "The spirit of the Lord is upon me . . . to proclaim release for the prisoners, to let the broken victims go free." Had Jesus not disturbed existing communities, he might not have been crucified. Herein lies our hope. We are confident that God is at work breaking, stretching, changing communities which are destructive, which limit us, which dehumanize us.

Let's look again to Acts for some guidelines, some clue for us as we respond to broken community. There is a time of grieving, a time of waiting, of healing, a time of expectation. But if we wait too long someone needs to say: "Why are you standing there? Get on with your work."

The apostles returned to the city, continuing in prayer, preaching, staying together, supporting each other, doing the work of their Lord. This weak community which deserted Jesus, which denied him, ended up being strong enough to be the foundation for the Christian church. We are still building on this foundation, moving on with new dreams and visions. We say with Loren Eiseley:

> The journey is difficult, immense, at times impossible, yet that will not deter some of us from attempting it. We cannot know all that has happened in the past, or the reason for all of

these events, any more than we can with surety discern what lies ahead. We have joined the caravan, you might say, at a certain point; we will still travel as far as we can, but we cannot in one lifetime see all that we would like to see or learn all that we hunger to know.*

We join the caravan and move on with the confidence that God is with us and herein lies our hope.

---

*Loren Eiseley, *The Immense Journey* (New York: Random House, 1957), p. 12.
Copyright © 1957 by Random House, Inc. Reprinted by permission.

Contributors

LaVonne Althouse: Pastor of Salem Lutheran Church, Philadelphia, Pennsylvania. Editor of *The Woman's Pulpit,* the official journal of the International Association of Women Ministers.

Karen Bloomquist: Pastor of Faith American Lutheran Church, Oakland, California.

Beatriz Melano Couch: Professor of Theology and Modern Literature at Union Theological Seminary, Buenos Aires, Argentina. Lectures and preaches frequently in the United States and in Latin America, and participates widely in ecumenical gatherings on these continents and Europe and Africa.

M. Nadine Foley, O. P.: Member of the General Council of the Adrian Dominican Sisters. Shared pastoral responsibilities with two priests and a layman at Drake Newman Community over a period of three years and preached regularly at Sunday liturgies.

Nancy Hardesty: Teaches American Church History at Candler School of Theology, Emory University, Georgia. A regular contributor to *Daughters of Sarah,* Christian feminist publication based in the evangelical tradition.

Monika K. Hellwig: Roman Catholic theologian, Associate Professor, Theology Department, Georgetown University, Washington, D.C. Preaches in Protestant and in Roman Catholic churches.

CARTER HEYWARD: Ordained Episcopal priest. Teaches at the Episcopal Divinity School, Cambridge, Massachusetts.

ALICE MANN: Ordained Episcopal priest. Associate at St. Asaph's Episcopal Church, Bala-Cynwyd, Pennsylvania.

SUE ANNE STEFFEY MORROW: Director of Admissions and Students' Affairs at Duke Divinity School.

ROSEMARY RADFORD RUETHER: Roman Catholic theologian. Georgia Harkness Professor of Applied Theology, Garrett-Evangelical Theological Seminary, Evanston, Illinois.

LETTY RUSSELL: Ordained in the United Presbyterian Church, U.S.A. Associate Professor of Theology, Yale Divinity School, New Haven, Connecticut. She was pastor in the East Harlem Protestant Parish, New York City, for ten years.

VALERIE RUSSELL: Assistant to the President of the United Church of Christ, with responsibility for mobilizing efforts around the issue of women in church and society. As a black woman, she also carries responsibility for minorities.

DOROTHEE SOELLE: Harry Emerson Fosdick Visiting Professor at Union Theological Seminary, New York City.

JEANETTE STOKES, M. Div.: Candidate, Duke Divinity School, Durham, North Carolina.

PHYLLIS TRIBLE: Samuel A. Hitchcock Professor of the Hebrew Language and Literature, Andover Theological School, Newton Center, Massachusetts.

BARBARA B. TROXELL: Ordained in the United Methodist Church. Associate Director of the Council on Ministries of the California-Nevada Conference. Has served in the parish ministry and in the student YWCA ministry.

PEGGY ANN WAY: Ordained in the United Church of Christ. Teaches at Vanderbilt School of Theology. Nashville, Tennessee.

CYNTHIA C. WEDEL: President (one of six) of the World Council of Churches. An Episcopal laywoman, she preaches almost every Sunday in one of many different churches.

HELEN GRAY CROTWELL: Ordained in the United Methodist Church. Associate Minister to Duke University, Durham, North Carolina.

DATE DUE

DEMCO 38-297